Making Money With Storage Auctions

by
Edward Busoni

Copyright Notice

Trademark Disclaimer

Copyright Acknowledgement

Legal Disclaimer

This publication provides information about the storage auction industry and includes references to certain legal and accounting principles. Although the author and the publisher believe that the included information is accurate and useful, nothing contained in this publication can be considered professional advice on any legal or accounting matter. You must consult a licensed attorney or accountant if you want professional advice that is appropriate to your particular situation.

Table Of Content

Introduction

I first heard about mini-storage auctions when I was in high school. The idea intrigued me a great amount. My parents loved going to garage sales on weekends and I had received a good education in that hobby. Now here I was presented with a variant. For sale, was a large amount of household items such as one would find at a garage sale, except you could buy everything in the garage for one rock bottom price.

It took me several years to actually go to a storage auction. I work late at night and I hate getting up early. This meant that I missed most auctions. As a rule they are held early in the morning. However, I finally attended an auction and it was a truly rewarding experience.

This was my first auction and I could tell that a lot of the people that were there were pros. They did this all the time, knew each other and knew what to expect. I knew nothing and was intimidated. This particular auction was a "piece out" auction where individual items are taken out of the storage unit and each item is auctioned off individually. I finally started making some bids and quickly became more comfortable. At this auction, a cable company's property was being auctioned off. I wound up buying eight spools of copper networking cable. My winning bid was a paltry $12. On the way home from the auction I stopped by a metal recycler where I had taken scrap metal before. I sold the copper wire there for almost $90! This blew me away. For an investment of $12 and an hour of my time, I had made a profit of $80. At the time I worked as a waiter and that was a night's worth of tips.

This really got me thinking. If this kind of money could be made with $12, what could $500 do? I was used to investing and had an investment portfolio and wondered if storage auctions could be an "alternative" investment that paid a much higher return. I did some further experimenting, bought some more items, sometime individual items and sometimes whole lockers. I made money. The return on investment was great. When I did not make money, I at least broke even and had some fun going though all the stuff I had bought. I formed a Limited Liability Corporation and bought a van and decided to turn this into a profitable hobby.

In the pages that follow this introduction, I am going to tell you how I do what I do and what I have learned while I have been doing it. I will tell you what I have done that has worked for me and I will tell you about mistakes I have made. This information is based entirely on my personal experience. I have no business degree; in fact I have no degree at all.

However, I have made money in these ventures and perhaps you can benefit from this information as well.

Before we get started, I need to insert a customary warning. The information presented in these pages is based on personal experience. While every effort has been made to ensure that this information is factual and correct, none of this information is to be considered expert advice. Before making decisions of a business, legal or financial nature, you are strongly encouraged to seek professional advice that is qualified and relevant to your personal situation.

All that being said, let's dive right in and get to the fun part – how to make money with storage auctions.

-Edward Busoni

Chapter 1
Introduction to Storage Auctions

Mini Storage Parks

America has a lot of stuff. People and families frequently have need for more space than they have in their homes. Businesses are no exception to this. Often times a business will need extra space for inventory or equipment. To answer this need, every city in America is dotted with storage parks that offer tenants access to storage space in garage like units for a monthly fee.

These can be very useful businesses. I have rented storage lockers at several points in my life. I had been forced to move out of my apartment at one point due to flooding and needed a place to put my stuff while I got things sorted out and rented another apartment. I have a friend who used these parks to store equipment for his business venture. Essentially he used the locker as a warehouse for supplies. I even know a man who is continuously restoring classic cars. He rents a storage space and uses it as a workshop for this hobby. All of his tools and equipment are in this space. For electricity he uses either a single outlet provided by the storage park, or uses a small generator he keeps there for the space as well.

Storage parks are often owned by investment companies known as "Real Estate Investment Trusts". These companies operate in a similar fashion to mutual funds. Essentially they take in money from smaller investors and place it in a communal pool. Using this communal pool of money, the companies invest in real estate instead of stocks. Some of these companies invest in large malls and office buildings, however, many of them invest in storage parks. These companies often have operations across the country.

You can rent storage spaces in many different sizes. The smallest spaces are generally a 5 foot by 5 foot space. These are similar in size to a closet. Sizes are not limited and for the right amount of money, any size can be rented. The largest that I have seen to date is a 25 foot by 25 foot space. This is an enormous space that is about the size of a single floor in a suburban home. Common sizes are 5'x5', 5'x10', 10'x10', 10'x15', 10'x20', and 20'x20'.

Rents for these storage spaces are determined by the amount of space that you are renting and the access to the space, as well as real estate costs in the city where the space is located. A space that will allow you to drive up to it will cost more in rent than an equally sized unit that is located inside of a building and will need to be accessed by an elevator.

What Is The Auction Process?

Unfortunately, storage companies are periodically forced to auction off the contents of their units. This occurs when people do not pay the rent as agreed and violate their rental contracts. The actual "foreclosure" process is a long, detailed process governed by the laws of the state that the storage company is operating in and can often take months.

Generally the first step in the foreclosure process that occurs immediately once the rent is past due, is called an "overlock" . This involves the storage company placing one of their locks on the storage unit. The tenant will not have a key to this lock and it will effectively prevent them from removing any of their possessions from the unit. A notice will also be placed on the unit informing the tenant that this step has occurred and that rent must be paid immediately. Breaking the lock and entering the unit is considered a crime and is punishable by law.

Most of the times that an "overlock" happens, the tenant will pay the bill and things return to normal. Even I have been late on a rental bill and had this first step in foreclosure occur. However, it also happens that people do not return and realize that this has occurred. Sometimes the bill remains unpaid and the tenant does not contact the storage company to make any arrangements.

When this happens, the process continues and will ultimately end in an auction. The company will send certified letters to the tenant's address that was provided at the time of rental and make every effort to contact them and alert the tenant to the fact that rent has not been paid. Many people are not in the habit of going to their storage units on a regular basis and things happen in life. Perhaps a financial manager was fired and their replacement was not aware of this financial obligation. This happens. In addition to attempting to contact the tenant through all the information supplied when the rental form was filled out the storage company will place ads in the local newspapers stating that the contents of a particular unit will be auctioned off at a certain date and time. This is done to make every last effort to allow the tenant to come and reclaim their goods. Perhaps the tenant has moved. If they have moved and did not get the certified letter, the newspaper ad will possibly reach them or someone they know will let them know about the impending auction. If this does occur, they can stop the auction by paying off the bill. This again will result in them being able to remove their stuff or begin to pay the bill regularly again. This frequently occurs.

If all of these means of getting the bill paid fail, the contents of the storage locker will be auctioned off to the highest bidder.

Why do auctions happen?

Auctions happen for the simple reason that storage companies are "for profit" companies. They make their money by renting the real estate they own to people. If the rent is not paid they are not making any money. It is not that they are simply not receiving any money, they are actually losing it. Real estate has costs as do all businesses. Property taxes have to be paid whether or not the rent is being paid. Also, the company has to pay electricity and garbage bills. Lastly, the storage companies have employees whose salaries will be paid regardless of the fact that rent is not being paid. To fix this situation, the company needs to get the stuff out of the unit and rent it to a tenant who will pay the bill. This is accomplished with the auction process and it serves two purposes.

First, under the terms of the rental agreement that every tenant signs the property in the unit is pledged as collateral for the rent. Once the bill is not paid, this property becomes the property of the storage company. It can be sold and the proceeds of the sale go to help cover any debt that remains unpaid. This helps to limit the financial losses of the storage company from the bad tenant.

The other purpose that is served is, by selling the goods at a low price to a third party, the storage company finds someone who will remove all of the stuff from the unit. A frequent rule at storage auctions is that you are responsible for removing EVERYTHING from a unit. Also, you are rarely given access to the storage company's dumpsters. If, you do gain access, go wild! It is much cheaper than going to the dump. This ultimately means that the disposal costs to the storage company are completely eliminated at the same time part of the outstanding debt is paid.

Why People Don't Pay The Rent

The property that is left behind in storage lockers can be sold for any number of reasons. There are four main reasons that I have encountered. These four are financial difficulty, moving, death and business failure.

In the case of financial troubles, a person frequently can not afford to pay the rent. Financial difficulty can strike for many reasons. Divorce is a very common cause of money troubles in America today as is credit card debt. Either one of these problems can cause weakness in a person's finances very quickly. People decide which bills to pay and which to ignore. Mortgage, car payments and utilities all take priority over storage rent. As a result, people stop paying these first. This can quickly lead to a storage unit foreclosure.

Moving can be another cause for storage auctions. People may have moved and left items in storage with the intention of returning. They may have gotten a better offer in the new city and decided to stay where they moved. If this occurs, it may not occur to them to tell the storage company where they have moved. They may simply decide the items in storage are not worth bothering with and they may simply abandon them and stop paying the bill. This is a frequent occurrence. I have seen units that were rented by a moving company. The invoices to the customer were still in there! Someone had sent their stuff from Florida with a moving company and had failed to pay the bill. When this happened, the moving company had stopped paying the bill to the storage company and a lot of very nice items went into foreclosure and were finally sold at auction.

Another possibility is that when they moved, they did not update their address with the storage company. In the event of a problem with payment, they cannot be contacted to remedy the situation. If that happens, the tenant will not know there is a problem and will not be able to fix it before the unit is auctioned off.

Sadly, in this world, people die. If a person is renting a storage locker and dies, it is possible that their next of kin will not know about the storage until and will not keep up the payments. When this happens the unit will go into foreclosure and will ultimately result in an auction. It is also possible that a person's next of kin will know about a person's left behind belongings and choose to abandon them. To many people this is easier than picking through many items that may have a lot of emotional baggage attached to them.

The last cause of storage locker auctions that I have seen is business failure. Many businesses make use of storage facilities to store inventory or equipment. I have seen a 10'x20' locker filled to the ceiling with cable receivers and computers.

When a business stops operating it is usually caused by two factors. One is that it has run out of money and the other is business mismanagement. Either one of these can cause a business to fail to pay its storage bill or often it is, again, simply easier to abandon the equipment than try to sell it off.

Is It Wrong To Profit From Storage Auctions?

Many people will think that they are a vulture for going to storage auctions. They feel that they are profiting from other people's pain, misery and suffering. This thought deserves a little exploring.

Yes, it is possible that you will make money from attending a storage auction. Yes, also, the auction may be a result of some misfortune in a person's life. You should come to grips with both of these facts before going to an auction.

This was uncomfortable for me when I first started and then I had several thoughts that did offer me comfort. First, you are not buying the property from the person in difficulty. You will be buying the property from the storage company. They have already seized the stuff and they are the ones selling it off. These items will be sold one way or the other.

The other fact that brings me comfort is that the person or business, whose property was seized, lost their items because they failed to honor a contract and failed to stop the foreclosure process.

The storage company is required by law to offer a number of chances for a tenant to stop the foreclosure process. Many letters will be mailed to them and notices will have been placed in the newspapers. Also, the storage company has a financial interest in having a tenant pay off their debt rather than selling the items at auction. Often times a tenant will have a debt of several hundred dollars to the storage company. At auction, this unit may only fetch $1 (I have seen this happen) and this represents and enormous loss to the storage company. It is in their interest to have a tenant pay the debt and they will be willing to work with tenants. Auctions only occur as a last resort when someone has been given lots of chances to pay their bill. I have seen managers delay an auction for thirty minutes just to let a tenant pay their bill at the last possible moment.

How Can You Benefit From Storage Auctions?

You can benefit greatly from storage auction. Let's face it. There are lots of really good things inside storage units. A short list includes:

- Furniture
- Electronics including stereos, DVD players, and televisions
- Antiques
- Cars
- Appliances such as refrigerators and washer/dryers
- Collectibles such as sports cards
- Records, tapes, CDs and DVDs
- Hand and power tools
- Books
- Bicycles
- Clothing
- Computers
- Sports equipment such as snowboards
- Beds
- Guns
- Jewelry
- Valuable Scrap Metal
- Boats
- Musical Instruments

This is really a short list. Essentially, anything that people can buy and own, they will store as well. In the event of an auction, all of this stuff can be yours at extremely low prices prices. Now, when I say rock bottom prices I really mean pennies on the dollar. It is not uncommon to see 10'x20' units sell at auction for $1.

The first way that storage auctions can benefit you is as a business opportunity. If you are buying a truckload of property for a dollar, there is a good chance that you can sort through and resell many of the items for a higher price. This can result in a very health profit margin. In fact, the profit margin can easily be 3 or 4 figures (such as 500%) depending on what type of treasures you may inadvertently have bought. There are all kinds of stories about the weird and valuable items that people have bought without even knowing it. You could be the next one to strike it rich.

You can also benefit from auctions as a way to buy all kinds of useful and needed things for next to nothing. In units I have bought, I have found nice jackets that I wear, microwaves that cook my popcorn on movie nights, jewelry my wife wears, tools that fix my car, art that decorates my home, carpets on my floors, and televisions I watch. This is not an exhaustive list. Essentially any type of item that you need can be found for next to nothing. It is possible that you will never have to pay retail or even wholesale again with the prices that you can find at storage auctions.

Another way that you can benefit is through giving. Many of the items in storage units can be used by other people but may not be of immediate use to you. You also may not be able to sell the items without trouble. However, you can donate the items to charity. Here the items can be sold or used by the charity. Many charities operate thrift stores and will have a much easier time selling items where you might have difficulty. Examples of items like this are clothing, silverware and picture frames.

Another way that donating the item to charity can benefit you is from the tax deduction you can take from it. Each time you donate items to charity, you can lower your taxable income by the value of the item as set by The Internal Revenue Service's rules. This in turn lowers the amount of money you pay in taxes. This can make donating to charity a win-win situation. Now, tax preparation can be a complicated area, so before donating and claiming deductions, talk with a qualified tax preparer and ask their advice.

Chapter 2
Setting Up an Auction Business

In the last chapter I described several ways that storage auctions can benefit you. We talked about acquiring personal goods at significant discounts, donating items to charity to help others and taking a tax write off, and reselling the items in the storage units for a profit. I use all three of these strategies but the remainder of this book will focus on going to storage auctions as a for profit business operation.

Before you start going to auctions and buying lots of great stuff, you should set up your business. Going to auctions and buying things before your business is in place is like putting the cart before the horse. This chapter is going to discuss all the steps and decisions that I made before I started going to auctions as a business. Now, again, these are decisions that I made. They were appropriate to my personal situation and financial circumstances. If you want to follow the path I chose and start an auction business, you would be well served to seek professional advice before starting. I did. In setting up the LLC I ultimately chose as my business structure I contracted an attorney to draw up my articles of incorporation. I also work with an accountant/ tax preparer whose advice I seek on tax planning. All that being said, let's get started.

Goals

Before I started my auction business, I needed to assess my goals. I work full time now and I was working full time then. As such I decided that the business I was planning would need to be on a part time basis. This meant that I would need to be able to do it when it was convenient to me and did not interfere with my job.

This type of decision making is important even though it may seem simple at first glance. Many of the people that attend storage auctions as part of a business do so as a means to provide themselves with store inventory. They operate antique, curio, pawn or thrift stores. They rent or own store space. Based on my need keep the business "part time" this type of setup would not work for me.

If you want to start an auction business, you should do some similar thinking. You need to examine your life and decide how much time you can devote to this enterprise. Do you take vacations that would make it hard for you to operate a storefront? Do you have frequent family obligations that would make it hard to go to auctions? When do you work? Most auctions are held during normal business hours, early in the morning on a weekday and will be hard to get to if you work during banker's hours. Think about all of these questions and give serious thought to this matter. Be honest with yourself. If you are unrealistic now, you may pay a great deal for it later.

Money, Money, Money

Starting a business takes money. This is true of any type of business you may choose to start, and it was true of my situation. However, storage auctions are a very financially friendly business to start.

I have said so far that you can buy storage units at auction for as low as a dollar in many cases. That is one of the reasons I decided to start the business that I did – it was cheap to start.

I only allowed $500 to fund my enterprise in the beginning. This was my "bank roll". This was to be the maximum amount I would invest in a purchase at any point. It still is a matter of fact and I have yet to break that rule.

You should decide on a magic number for yourself. It really depends on the amount of money you make and what you are comfortable investing in this type of a scenario. You should consider storage auctions as high risk investments. It is entirely possible that you will buy a lemon and loose your investment. However, you can get started for a small sum that will not require you to take out a loan or mortgage the house. All that being said, remember the Golden Rule of Investing. That is, never invest more than you can afford to lose. Storage auctions should always be considered speculative, high risk investments and should be treated accordingly.

Forming Your Business

Once you have decided that you would like to operate a storage auction business, you need to form a business and set it up for success. To do that you need to create an entity, obtain licenses, open bank accounts and all the other minor details that go into starting a business.

Your Business Entity

The structure of your business is one of the most important decisions that you need to make during the preparation phase of your business. The decisions you make at this point have large impacts on taxes, risk management, and estate planning as well as liability.

These are decisions that will most likely require professional advice regarding your state regulations and your personal situation. Now, hopefully, where business expenses are concerned you are careful with your financial resources. Professional advice is one of the areas that you need to be willing and prepared to spend some money. The outcome of these consultations, have huge implications on your business and you want to make sure that you receive qualified guidance. Do not think of attorney's fees as expenses, but as investments in the financial health and security of your new company and your personal wealth.

The following explanations are very basic and are intended to give you only the most general understanding of various business structures and risks. Many books are available that address the issues of starting a business and each particular business structure in depth. Your local library can be a wonderful, inexpensive resource to learn all that you need on business structures before you consult an attorney. The more prepared and educated you are before walking into your attorney's office, the easier and cheaper the process will be.

Sole Proprietorships

By far the simplest form of business that anyone can undertake is that of the sole proprietorship. What this entails is an individual doing business as an individual. The individual needs to register a business name with the state's corporations division, but that is about all that is required. There is usually a simple form to fill out and a negligible fee. Many states even allow you to do this online with a credit or debit card. There may be some additional rules or regulations that vary by state, but the whole process can easily be done in an afternoon.

In addition to filing papers with the state, you may need to apply for an Employer Identification Number (EIN) from the IRS, open a company bank account, buy an insurance policy, etc. All of these activities will be carried out in your name. That is to say you, John Smith, will sign your name and social security number on all business documents. You will also be personally responsible for all debts and liabilities of your company.

That last element is one that deserves further explanation. A sole proprietorship exposes its operator to a significant lawsuit risk. There is no limited liability provisions like those offered by the corporate business structures. In the event that someone is damaged by the activities of your business, your personal property and assets can be used to settle the debts that arise from any judgments. Because of this rather large risk to my private assets I never considered this business model. In order to help protect my family and wealth, I sought out the protection of an LLC.

Partnerships

Partnerships are very similar to sole proprietorships in that they are simple to form and require only the smallest amount of paperwork, if any. In some cases a partnership can even be formed, in the eyes of the law, without the knowledge of the partners simply by the existence of a contract between participants. An additional similarity to sole proprietorships is the fact that partners in the partnership may be personally responsible for the debts and liabilities of the partnership. This, again like a sole proprietorship, will put at risk your personal assets in the event of mismanagement or lawsuit. Since the startup and operating costs of an auction business are so small, there is little reason to consider a partnership.

Corporations

The concept of the corporation is one of the developments that lead to the Industrial Revolution and the modern world we enjoy today. Essentially, filing articles of incorporation creates a new legal entity. This entity is owned indirectly by individuals known as shareholders. This legal entity has the ability to carry out business just as an individual would, but with added benefits.

One of benefits is that a corporation helps to protect personal assets. That is to say, outside of personal negligence, the only money and assets that you put at risk are the money or assets that you have invested in the corporation. This is an invaluable benefit and is the main reason most businesses are formed as a corporation.

There are several other ways in which a corporation's liability protection can be pierced. A short list of these behaviors is:

- Commingling
- Undercapitalization
- Illegal activities
- Failure to comply with corporate regulations

Commingling occurs when your personal assets and your corporation's assets are inseparable and non distinct. This occurs when you and your corporation share a bank account or when you sign your personal name on corporate documents without a qualifying title. Commingling is a very serious concern and is something to discuss in detail with your attorney at the time of incorporation. Their advice can easily eliminate this risk

Undercapitalization occurs when a corporation exists without the means to carry on its business in an independent manner. This occurs when the corporation owns nothing and has no cash on hand. This is a smaller concern than commingling but again should be discussed with your filing attorney at the time of incorporation. You will need to keep your corporation adequately funded at all times.

It is not in the interests of the state to protect your personal assets from lawsuit in conjunction with illegal activities. Corporations that engage in illegal activities put the personal assets of their shareholders at risk. This is easily defended against by making sure that your corporation complies with all laws and conducts its business in a respectable, legal manner at all times.

The last of the mistakes one can make that will invalidate their corporate liability protection is a failure to comply with regulations. All this means, is that your state has rules governing corporations and you need to adhere to them religiously. In most states this simply means writing an operating agreement, choosing a name, and filing articles of incorporation. Annual filings will also need to be prepared. Again you will need to consult a local professional regarding the rules of you state before proceeding. In exchange for a small fee, many law firms will act as the registered agent of your corporation. They will prepare and file all of the required documents for you and keep them up to date. The fee for this is usually reasonable and will eliminate the concern of maintaining your documents altogether.

Survivorship

Another one of the benefits of a corporate business structure is survivorship. When you create a corporation you create a distinct and separate legal entity from yourself. In the event of the death of a shareholder, such as you, the stock in a corporation reverts to the shareholder's heir as specified in their will or as determined by a probate court. The corporate entity is not affected by the death of one of its shareholders. This means that your business can be around long after your passing and can be a convenient tool used for estate planning.

Pass Through Taxation

Before discussing some of the various corporate types, pass through taxation needs to be explained. Pass through taxation means that the profits and losses of the corporation pass through the corporation, tax free, to the shareholders. Once the shareholders have received the profits and losses they are included in their personal tax returns. Under this system, profits are only taxed once. This system is impossible with a "C Corporation". Pass through taxation is only allowed by the IRS for "S Corporations" and "LLCs" as of this writing.

UBI Number

If you form your company as a corporation the secretary of state where you reside, will provide your company with a unique number known as a UBI Number. UBI stands for Universal Business Identification Number. This number will uniquely identify your business and will be required in many business dealings such as opening a bank account. This number is a publicly available number and is not to be confused with the more useful, and necessary of protection, Employer Identification Number.

If you choose to operate as a sole proprietorship, you will not receive a UBI. Instead you will use your Social Security number as a means to identify your business.

Types of Corporations

The following sections list very brief descriptions of several types of corporate structures along with relevant strengths and weaknesses. This information is intended only to point you in the right direction when doing further research into the area of corporations. These pages will also allow you to ask the right questions when meeting with your attorney.

C Corporations

C Corporations are what most people think of when they think of corporations. Many publicly traded corporations exit as C Corporations. A C Corporation allows the type of asset protection that any corporation does. There is no limitation on the number of investors that a C Corporation can have.

There is one significant downside to C Corporation that makes it particularly unsuitable to the small business owner. A C Corporation does not allow pass through taxation. As such a C Corporation will have to file a separate tax return and pay taxes on its profits. Once its profits have been taxed those profits can be distributed to its shareholders and can be subject to additional taxation. All of this overhead and possible additional tax is often more than a small business owner can afford to deal with. For a storage auction business, it makes far more sense to form as an S Corporation or an LLC.

S Corporations

S corporations were an improvement over C corporations with the small business owner in mind. The most attractive feature of S corporations is that they do allow pass through taxation while providing the asset protection of any corporation. S corporations do have one downside. There are often limits on the amount of shareholders permitted under an S corporation. When starting an auction business, you will often find that you are the only, or one of few shareholders. This is fine at first and is even fine forty years into your business as you are retiring. However, there is no logical reason to limit the amount of investment that your business can receive by limiting the number of shareholders you can have. Who knows where your business adventures will lead? The next corporate type solves all of these problems and is the form that is recommended by many professionals for any small business these days.

Limited Liability Corporations (LLC)

Limited Liability Corporations offer the best of both worlds and offers the best business structure for a small business, in my opinion. Limited Liability Corporations have no limits on the number of potential shareholders and offer the same liability protections as offered by S corporations and C corporations, as well as, pass through taxation.

One thing to note is that the Limited Liability Corporation structure is a fairly new business structure. Most states did not have this structure until after 1990. That being said professional (attorneys and accountants) awareness of this structure is still growing and laws governing this structure are still evolving. This is a great reason to do your homework. Get familiar with the requirements and advantages in your state before you contract a professional to do your paperwork. This will save you time and money and will greatly help in discussing your needs and goals with your counsel.

Forming a Corporation

Once you have selected the corporate structure that you believe is appropriate, it is time to talk to an attorney. Many paralegals and accountants will also be willing to file corporate papers for your new company. Many computer programs also exist to help with this process and you can even write your own operating agreement. However, in a matter as serious as personal wealth protection, the premier advice of an attorney is recommended.

To find an attorney, you can ask friends and family for referrals, use the yellow pages, or you can take advantage of your state's bar association. The bar association is the professional association for attorneys in your state. Along with maintaining professional standards these groups also provide referral services as well as information about specific attorneys in your area. The bar association is a great place to begin your search for legal counsel.

The first and most important document that is required to form a corporation is called an "Operating Agreement". This document spells out in black and white all the particulars of the corporation. These details include but are not limited to formation, accounting, rights and duties of shareholders, management, profit distribution, taxes, and dissolving the corporation. Also listed in this document are the forming shareholders, the management, main offices, effective date and a registered agent.

The registered agent is a shareholder or hired individual or company that will be responsible for receiving and answering all official communications for the corporation and preparing and filing all documents as required by the state. You can undertake this role yourself; however, in many cases for a small annual fee the law firm that does your filing will also act as your agent. The fee is very reasonable and the firm will automatically keep your annual reports and other filings up to date.

Once you have consulted with your attorney and have decided on a corporate type and your attorney has all the necessary information, you are done for a while. Your attorney will prepare your documents and send them to you for your signature. Once you have signed them you will send them to your attorney who will forward them to the secretary of state. Your attorney will most likely also submit the corporate filing fee (this can range from $50 to $500) and bill you for it later.

If everything is in order with your documents you will ultimately receive a certificate of formation listing the official name of your company along with the effective date and the UBI number. Once you have this you are the manager and shareholder of a corporation.

Employer Identification Number

An Employer Identification Number (EIN) is very similar to a Social Security Number. However, the numbered individual is generally a corporation, partnership or sole proprietorship. Your company's EIN will be used on all official documents such as tax filings, bank accounts, insurance policies and credit applications. This number will be necessary before you can attend to any of these mentioned tasks.

You will need to have formed your corporation or filed your sole proprietorship/partnership documents before requesting an EIN. To request an EIN you can either apply online, or fill out and mail an IRS Form SS-4. The form can be downloaded from www.irs.gov or you can request one from your local IRS Office. There is no fee. If your application is approved you will be mailed your EIN in several weeks. You will need to protect this number just as you would a Social Security Number from identity thieves.

Form **SS-4** (Rev. February 2008) Department of the Treasury Internal Revenue Service	**Application for Employer Identification Number** (For use by employers, corporations, partnerships, trusts, estates, churches, government agencies, Indian tribal entities, certain individuals, and others.) ▶ See separate instructions for each line. ▶ Keep a copy for your records.	OMB No. 15 EIN

Type or print clearly.

1 Legal name of entity (or individual) for whom the EIN is being requested	

2 Trade name of business (if different from name on line 1)	3 Executor, administrator, trustee, "care of" name

4a Mailing address (room, apt., suite no. and street, or P.O. box)	5a Street address (if different) (Do not enter a P.O. bc
4b City, state, and ZIP code	5b City, state, and ZIP code

6 County and state where principal business is located	

7a Name of principal officer, general partner, grantor, owner, or trustor	7b SSN, ITIN, or EIN

8a Type of entity (check only one box)
- ☐ Sole proprietor (SSN) _____
- ☐ Partnership
- ☐ Corporation (enter form number to be filed) ▶ _____

- ☐ Estate (SSN of decedent) _____
- ☐ Plan administrator (SSN) _____
- ☐ Trust (SSN of grantor) _____
- ☐ National Guard ☐ State/local gov

A Form SS-4 from the IRS will allow you to quickly and easily apply for an Employer Identification Number.

Once you have established your business, you will need to deal with some red tape before you can begin doing business. These are not especially difficult chores but will need to be done correctly to prevent headaches in the future, and risk to your personal assets and your young company.

Business Licenses

The first thing you need to attend to once you have formed your company is a business license. This basically gives your company permission to conduct business within a particular area. The best place to begin researching business licenses will be with your state's business division. The US Small Business Association (www.sba.org) is also a wealth of information regarding licenses.

You may be required to obtain a license at the state, county and city level. You may only be required to obtain a license if your gross sales are above a certain point. Fees for business licenses are reasonable and can be tax deductible. You will most likely need to renew your license annually. You can apply for your initial license and renew online in many cases using your credit or debit card. Once you have received your license, frame it and place it prominently wherever you conduct your business.

Opening Company Bank Accounts

Your business will be very limited in terms of what it can do until you have opened a company bank account. Most commercial banks will open business checking accounts for any type of business. Some credit unions will only open accounts for sole proprietorships. You will need to call before going into the bank or you can ask one of the customer service representatives. They will be happy to answer any questions you have.

Before walking into the bank, however, you should get all of the necessary original documents together in a file. A little organization will make things much easier. In most cases you will need the following documents:

- Certificate of Formation or
- Assumed Business Name Filing
- Operating Agreement
- UBI Number (This is on your certificate of formation.)
- EIN Number (This will be provided from the IRS in a letter.)

The first account that you should open is a simple business checking account. Look for one without a minimum balance or monthly fee. This will help your business keep costs low. You will need to provide some sort of initial deposit in addition to the documents listed above. If you are operating as a corporation, ask your attorney as to how you should provide this initial deposit. This will prevent any problems with commingling.

In addition to opening the account you will need to order checks as well. These will be very useful as receipts and will be helpful in tracking expenses. You should only purchase the least expensive checks that are offered or try to get free ones, but you should get checks with carbon copies. There is no need to waste corporate money on designer checks. This money can be better invested in your young company's operations. Your checks should have your company name, address, and perhaps phone numbers on them. Unless you are operating as a sole proprietorship or your name is part of your corporate identity, your personal name should not appear on your checks.

Once you have opened your checking account, you will be able to open corporate brokerage accounts and accounts with other financial companies. These will help you manage any excess cash. You will also be able to begin auction purchases for your company and use the check copies as receipts. Later, these will be used for equipment depreciation when tax time rolls around.

Sales Taxes

With very few exceptions, if you engage in commerce in the United States, you will be required to remit sales tax revenue to state and municipal governments.

The regulations governing sales vary by state and you will need to do homework concerning your particular situation. To find out what is required, contact your local sales tax bureau. If you are unsure of where to find this agency, start with your state's department of revenue. In most cases, the agency that is responsible for collecting sales tax revenue in your area will happily mail you a comprehensive packet containing all the forms necessary to begin collecting and remitting sales tax. Governments love companies that want to pay taxes. These forms along with helpful brochures may also be available online as well.

Conclusion

After reading this chapter you should have a better idea of what type of business you want your auction business to be. As was said before, this was not an exhaustive discussion of the subject of business formation and organization. If you are serious about forming a company, I strongly recommend paying a visit to your local library or bookstore. There, you are guaranteed to find many volumes on these complicated subjects. Read through several of these to more fully acquaint yourself with the subject. Only then, once you have done your homework should you go to an attorney's office to formally begin the process.

Chapter 3
Finding and Going to Auctions

Finding Auctions

You cannot attend an auction and buy fabulous things at prices that are a steal if you do not know when and where the auctions are going to be held. So, as a matter of course, you are going to need to find some auctions before you start.

I have done this in several ways. The first of the methods I have used is keeping an eye on the local newspaper. As I have mentioned before, as a part of the foreclosure process, storage companies are required to post legal advertisements in newspapers alerting people that they are in financial arrears and that they have one last opportunity to pay the bill and redeem their property before it is sold at auction. They are also required to post when and where the property will be auctioned off as well. This has provided me with a wealth of information.

Most newspapers will have a section close to the beginning of their classified section titled something like "Public Notices" or "Auctions". If it is not right at the beginning, consult the classified index of the newspaper to find a similarly titled section.

Once I have located the section of the classifieds that I am looking for, I start scanning through and looking at the ads. Depending on the size of the city served by the newspaper, there may be only a few or there may be many auction notices. Where I live, on any given day there are at least five or six ads. I look at these carefully and pick out a few bits on information.

First, I find out where the auction is. I still don't like getting up early and I am really not interested in driving out to the middle of nowhere for an auction that has only listed two units that may be auctioned off. I usually do not drive more than 25 miles or so to an auction. If you buy a large unit and have to make several trips to move everything, you will pay a fortune in gas.

The next piece of information that I look at is how many units may be auctioned off. I say "may" because not all listed units will be auctioned off. Remember, the purpose of the ad is to alert people to the fact their property will be sold and to give them a chance to redeem it. Invariably, some of the people whose names are listed in the ad will see it and pay their bill. This will remove their unit from the potential auction. When I look at an ad, I count the amount of units that may be sold and reduce that number by half. Then, based on that number, I decide if there are enough units for sale to warrant going to the auction. If there is only one unit for sale at a storage facility that is 30 miles away, I will most likely pass. If on the other hand, there is an auction that has listed 20 units in the paper (meaning that there will probably be at least 10 for auction) that is 30 miles away, it may be worth my time to go check it out. These are rules that I use and you are welcome to develop your own.

The next source of information about auctions is from the storage facilities themselves. Many of these businesses maintain websites. These websites can offer information about upcoming auctions. It is in the interest of these businesses to publicize their auctions. In some states, there are minimum participant requirements for an auction to be legal. If not enough people show up, the storage facility must keep the property, taking up space that could be earning rent or pay someone to haul it away.

Look for a link that mentions "Auctions". If you cannot find it, you will certainly be able to find contact information for the company itself. Give them a call and tell them that you are interested in attending their auctions. Most of them will be happy to provide you with a time and location of the next upcoming auction. Several of the companies I have dealt with have provided me with calendars for the rest of the year. These are extremely handy. With them, I do not even need to keep an eye on the paper. Instead, I simply consult the calendar and instantly know the date, time and location of many auctions. If you can get your hands on one of these make sure you hang on to it. When speaking to the staff at the storage facility, ask if you can be put on any mailing list they maintain. These are an excellent resource. They will mail you a small postcard shortly before the next auction is scheduled. This way, when an auction is coming up, you will have to search no farther than your mailbox.

The last place that you can find auctions is from professional auctioneers. Some auctioneers can be found in the phonebook. However, many of these will only be known from word of mouth. Most of the auctioneers that I am aware of, I have encountered because they conducted auctions that I attended. Auctioneers will generally advertise their upcoming auctions before an auction starts. Some of them will place flyers out with upcoming events and their contact information. I pick these up every time I find one and keep them in a special file. Also, ask for a business card. That way, I can keep tabs on their upcoming events through their websites.

The best way to keep all of the dates, times, and locations of all the auctions you will find is to keep a calendar. Go out to a local office supply store and pick one up. It should not cost you more than $10 and the organizational help that it offers will be well worth the price. I use one and can tell at a glance what is going on tomorrow or a month in advance and can decide based on this readily available information, which auctions I wish to attend.

Preparing For An Auction

Before actually going to a storage auction, you need to do some prep work. You need to make sure that you are setup and ready to go. If the auction moves from one location to another, you will not have any time to grab lunch, hit a cash machine, or get more batteries for your flashlight.

One thing I always do before an auction, especially if the auction moves from location to location, is make sure that I have proper directions. I will either plot a course on a map, or get directions from one of the online direction services. I also carry a book of maps in my car for the area where I live, that way, if my directions are incorrect, I can quickly fix the problem and not miss the auction. I would strongly suggest buying a detailed map of the area you will be working in and making sure that you know exactly how to use it.

The first thing that you should do is call the office where the auction will be held. I do this during business hours the day before the auction is to be held. Many auctions are held before or just as the office opens. This means that there will not be enough time for you to call and confirm the day of the auction. You want to confirm all of the details you have found either in the paper or on the company's website. I ask them if they are indeed having an auction the next day. It is possible that everyone is paid up and the auction is canceled. If they are having an auction, I ask them how many units are for sale. Again, based on this information and where the auction will be held I reconsider whether or not I want to attend. The last bit of info that I need, is whether I can pay for the auction with a business credit card or whether the auction terms are cash only.

If everything is good, and the auction is still on, I organize all the items that I will need. If the auction is cash only, I will go out and supply myself with cash. I generally take about $500 if the auction terms specify cash. Then, I make sure that I have plenty of padlocks. If you are the winner in one of the auctions, you will need to place you own lock on the unit to secure your new property. I generally remove my new property the day of the auction or the next day, so I do not have the highest security locks in most cases. If I plan to leave the stuff for a while I will supply a high security disc lock to help make sure everything is where I left it. It is sad to say but people do break in to storage units. They are either stealing their former property back or are just thieves looking for a fast buck. A disc lock with a hardened steel construction will help prevent the use of bolt cutters to enter your unit and steal your property.

Lastly I pack a bag with some items that I have found useful in the past. The first item that I make sure to pack is a "sun gun". This is a hand held high powered flashlight. These types of lights can be found at any hardware store. Mine cost me about $30. It was a little expensive for a flashlight, but making sure you have a reliable high powered flash light can help you spot all the treasures that other people might miss. Consider a flashlight a required piece of equipment that you should not get caught without.

A well made reliable spotlight style flashlight will be an essential tool when you go to storage auctions. I never attend an auction without one.

I also like to pack a set of tools. This includes:

- Hammer

- Soft hammer or mallet
- Pliers
- Screwdrivers (flat and Phillips)
- Knife or box cutter
- Set of Allen wrenches
- Ratchet set
- Tape measure

You can assemble all of these tools piece meal, or you can buy ready made tool sets in carrying cases that include all of these items and more. These sets are generally priced under $20. The last thing I always pack is a roll of heavy duty garbage bags. These can come in very handy when you are cleaning out a storage unit. Many people are not all that tidy when they pack things into storage. Garbage bags make it easier to get things in order before you remove them. I once bought a unit and filled 20 bags with clothing. The clothes were literally piled up without any boxes or trunks. Without the garbage bags it would have been much harder to truck them to a charity thrift store.

The Auction Process

Once you have gotten everything in order and confirmed that there is indeed an auction you can actually go and see what you can find.

I always leave early for an auction. I have many reasons for doing this. First, if you are slightly unsure of where the storage company is located, this allows you a time cushion if you get lost. It is also a good idea to show up early because you will need to fill out some paperwork before the auction starts.

This paperwork is used to provide your information to the storage company for use during the auction and on any legal documents that you will need to sign in the event you buy a unit. Generally, these documents ask for your company name, your name, address, phone number, and email. I always make sure to fill in my email address and phone number. Many storage companies maintain a buyers list based on this auction paperwork. Some will even give you an alert before an auction by either email or post.

If you are doing business as a corporation or LLC, talk to your attorney about what you should write down on the auction paperwork. Writing down your personal name when you are buying units for your corporation, could be considered commingling.

The final reason to show up early is to scope out the competition. You will usually have to wait before the auction starts, during this time you can meet and chat with other buyers. While everyone is in competition with each other, in my experience, many people are friendly. People in situations such as this are often very happy to trade war stories. Also, since most of these people will be in the business as well they may be able to offer you things you need. I know a buyer who bought his first service vehicle directly from another, more experienced, buyer. The seller had actually bought the van at another storage auction. The new guy got a useful van at a great price and I am certain that the seller made a healthy profit. Everyone won in this case.

Once it is time to start, the auction will get going. The auctioneer, often just the facility manager, will come out and tell you the terms of the auction. I have already mentioned that the auction can be either for the whole unit with everything in it or it will be a "piece out" auction where each item is auctioned off separately or in small lots in my experience, "piece out" auctions are fairly rare. In addition to this the auctioneer will tell you whether the auction will be out loud or if it will be a silent bid auction. A verbal auction is the type that most people think of when they hear the word auction. With this type, people call out their bids and you as a competitor can counter with your own. Everyone knows what everyone is bidding.

The other type of auction that is possible is a silent bid auction. With this type of auction each buyer is issued a piece of paper for each unit that is for sale. So, if there are five units, you will receive five forms. When the bidding commences, each bidder writes down their maximum bid. The papers are handed to the auctioneer and the winner is the buyer who wrote down the highest bid.

I much prefer a verbal auction to a silent one. With a silent bid, you have only one chance to bid. My instinct is generally to bid the lowest amount that I think will be accepted so I can make more money if I win. This is not helpful with a silent bid. With a silent bid I have to find a balance between offering too much, much more than any other buyer, and trying to low ball the storage company. When I do bid, I try to bid a "random" number. Many people will bid in amounts of $5 or $25. To outbid these people other buyers will often bid, say, $26. If people know your patterns they will find it easier to outbid you. What I do is bid something like $47 dollars or $116. These numbers have no real pattern and will help keep your game plan unpredictable and give you a better chance of winning the unit.

With a verbal auction I have a chance to up my bid as I determine it is necessary. I can see and hear what the other bidders are up to. Also, if no one is bidding, I can always throw out a token number like $1 and maybe get a great deal. When bidding in verbal auctions, I will increase my bid in units of $25 or $50. I do not try to go up in a bidding war by $1 or less. Many auctioneers will not appreciate this and the other buyers will find it irritating as well. You should never forget to courteous.

Once all the terms are out in plain sight and everyone is on the same page, the auction will start. The auctioneer will open the first unit and start taking everything out if it is a piece out or let everyone take a look if the auction if for the whole unit. Whole unit auctions are far more common, so for the rest of this discussion that is the auction type that I will be referring to.

Looking over all the stuff in the unit is the most important part of the auction. It is from here that you decide whether or not you want to buy the unit and how much you want to pay for it.

You will not be allowed to root through or move anything in the auction. You will only be allowed to look over what is in plain sight. This is where your flashlight becomes vitally important. You need a good light to be able to see. Many times, a mattress or something else large will be blocking the door and you will need your light to see through the cracks to what is behind it.

I always take my time and look things over very carefully. I peep through as many little cracks that I can and see what I can find with my light. I look and see if the items are in good condition. I check to see if things are clean and organized. Someone who has gone to a great deal of effort to box and wrap their property is doing so for a reason. Usually this means something of value. I saw a storage locker once that had a large padded package that no one could figure out. It turned out it was a carefully padded plasma television. I did not win that auction but the person who did made a lot of money with that one!

When at the auction, this is as good a view as you will get. You will not be allowed to search through any of this before bidding. You would not know it to look at it, but this unit contained many valuable items.

I also take a deep sniff. Does everything smell OK? Were the owners smokers? Did they own cats that urinated on everything? Taking a deep sniff can help you avoid buying a unit full of smelly junk that you will only have to truck to the dump.

I also carefully look for any items of value. This can be hard and subjective. What may be valuable to me and easily sold could be totally worthless to another buyer. Based on what I can see and what

I think those items are worth, I decide the maximum amount I will bid on a unit. This is a very subjective skill and is really up to you and your taste for risk, as well as your experience level.

Once everyone has had a chance to look the bidding will start. Stick to your guns and bid aggressively but do not go over the maximum amount you decided to bid. Some experienced buyers may throw their weight around and try to get you to pay more than a unit is worth by bidding the auction up. Don't let them push you around. If they want it more than you do, let them have it. There will be plenty of other auctions in the future and a little patience can be very rewarding. Plus, if they bid more than a unit is worth, and you walk away, they may think twice about doing that in the future.

Paying attention during the auction can benefit you a great deal. First, watch the other buyers. Watch what they do and what they buy. Think of this as a poker game and they are the other players. The more you observe them and learn how they conduct themselves, the better you will do. Also, pay attention to the items that are sold. I always watch and see what items are sold and what the units that contain them sell for. I carry a notebook with me and write down items that I see during the auction, if I do not know what they are worth. That way, after the auction, I can look for them online and in catalogs and determine their value for future auctions. This way I profit from experience.

When a bidder has won the auction they will be expected to immediately secure their new property with a lock. I always carry at least three padlocks with me when to accomplish this. If you win an auction and do not have a lock with you, some storage parks will loan you one. Other storage companies will immediately disqualify you and move to the next highest bidder. Make sure you always have locks!

That is the basic auction procedure. It will be repeated as many times as they have units to sell. If you are fortunate enough to win one of the units, you will need to put one of your locks on the unit. When every unit has been auctioned off, the winners will go to the office with the auctioneer and pay for their units. You will receive a receipt of some kind. If you do not make sure you ask and get one. These will be very useful come tax time (as we will discuss in a later chapter).

Once all of these procedures are taken care of, the stuff is yours. You will then need to clean out the storage unit as directed by the rules of the auction. In the next chapter we will talk about how I remove, transport and sort all of my new found treasures.

The Code Of Silence

Storage auctions are a bit of a secret. This may seem like an odd idea considering all the trouble and expense that the mini storage companies go to in publicizing their auctions to satisfy legal requirements. However, most people that you meet and talk to about storage auctions will not have the faintest idea what you are talking about until you have explained everything.

This is because there is a fortune auctioned off every month. By some estimates, tens of thousands if not hundreds of thousands of mini storage units are auctioned off to satisfy debts every month in this country. This is an absolutely immense amount of personal property. The people that know about storage auctions want to keep this secret under their hats. They do not want the vast majority of people out there realizing how much stuff can be bought for such little amounts of money.

This atmosphere may be very obvious when you go to your first auction. Many of the experienced buyers will be very familiar with each other and seem to be on very friendly terms with the auctioneers and storage staff. They may even seem to form a clique of experienced buyers that can leave you feeling like the new guy on the first day of high school. Don't let this atmosphere intimidate you. They were new once and look at them now. They are experienced and some day, if you stick with it, you will have the same wealth of experience. Also, take comfort in the fact that you have as much right to be at and participate in these auctions as anyone.

This may sound like a horror story, but it is not. While some buyers are cold, many of them, especially other novices like you will be very friendly.

Things I Avoid

There are several things that will make me walk away from a unit all together. First, if the unit is a lot of work, and I am busy that week I will generally pass. Examples of units that are a lot of work are those that are crammed floor to ceiling and go back for twenty feet with what appears to be totally unorganized junk.

Two other immediate red flags, to me personally, are mattresses and couches. Some people buy these all the time and I have in the past. I once saw a woman gleefully buy a unit that appeared to be filled with smelly old mattresses. She may have found some treasures behind them. I honestly do not know. However, from my experience, these two items are bulky hard to store items that are also hard to sell. You <u>can</u> sell them and make money, but it takes longer than other types of items. As a general rule, I avoid them because I believe they are inconvenient. Now, once I saw a unit with a couch, a mattress, and a 50" inch big screen TV. I did not have a truck at that point and the TV would have been hard to move. I decided to pass. The unit sold for $1. If I had had a truck, I would have definitely bid on it.

There are also some items that I view with caution. I will buy them, but I will not get carried away with the bidding. These items are safes, locked trunks, and new appliance or computer boxes. These could be filled with all kinds of treasures, but they are most often not. Think to yourself. When was the last time you bought a new plasma screen TV and put it right back into the box to put it in storage?

On the other hand, I have and know other buyers who have bought locked trunks and found really great stuff inside too.

Don't Bite Off More Than You Can Chew

I did not have the benefit of this book when I went to my first storage auction. My approach was simple trial and error. The first unit that I bought was enormous. It was ten feet by twenty feet, completely full to the ceiling with unorganized piles of stuff. I rented a moving truck and spent two days hauling everything back to where I would sort it. There was so much stuff that I had only had time to quickly unload and go back for more. I did not have time to organize the boxes at all.

When all was said and done, I had filled my garage to bursting. There was not even enough space to walk in there. I had to climb over and sneak around things to move. I was lucky that I had enough space because I had given no consideration to those requirements when I bought the unit; I had just wanted to buy something so badly. These days I am careful what I buy and I make sure that I have enough room for everything. When I first look at a unit, I always make sure I know the size of the unit and make sure I have space available. If a unit is just too big for me, I will pass and wait for something that is a better fit. When you are going to auctions, I advise using the same caution.

People Buying Back Their Own Property

In the states with which I am familiar, it is illegal for a person who is the renter of a foreclosed unit to buy it back at auction. This does not mean that it does not happen. Frequently people will send their friends and relatives to bid on their behalf. This is also not allowed by the terms of the auction, but, realistically, there is little the storage company can do to prevent it. They cannot do background checks on every buyer.

Spotting these people is not very difficult. They will show a very specific and targeted interest in one particular unit. They may ask when a specific unit or a specific person's items will be sold. This is an instant indicator. A normal auction buyer is not interested in just one unit. When the auction starts for the unit they are interested in, they will bid very aggressively.

When I see a situation like this, I will generally pass on bidding. The last thing I want to deal with is someone hassling me over buying their stuff. This is also forbidden by the rules of the auction but I prefer to skip the whole possible headache altogether.

Some buyers will see a situation like this and do just the opposite. They will bid back aggressively and try to drive the price of the unit up quickly. This is a strategy that you can employ as well, but I avoid it too.

Auctioneers will watch for these people as well. Sometimes, sadly, these people will bid and win an auction and then stay behind when the group has moved on. They will clean out all the valuable items and take off without paying for the unit. This is also highly illegal. If I ever see anything like this, I immediately alert the storage manager or auctioneer. They will put a stop to it quickly and appreciate the help.

Keep Your Records

If you purchase a unit at an auction, it is very important for you to keep any records that you are given after the sale. These are very important legal documents that you should keep safely somewhere. This documentation can take several forms. I have bought units from companies that provide you with rigorous documentation on several pages of professionally prepared legal documents. This documentation certifies that you bought a specific unit as the winner of a competitive bidding situation and will also list the price as well as your information including name, address and phone number. Other companies that I have purchased units from will supply you with a simple hand written receipt out of an office supply store receipt book. Either way, each time I buy a unit, I create a file for it and store all of the documents that I am given for that unit.

This may seem like being over cautious, however, in the event that a person appears and claims that you are in illegal possession of their items, you can always produce evidence that clearly states that you purchased these items legally after a lengthy foreclosure process was conducted by the storage company. This can be an important safeguard.

Conclusion

In this chapter, I presented several easy ways to find the storage auctions that are planned in your area. Also, we discussed what it will most likely be like at the auction itself. Armed with this information, you are ready to embark on your new auction career or hobby. Remember to be patient, if you do not win the first units you bid on, do not be discouraged, there is plenty for all and yours will come. Also remember to watch and listen, to learn while you are at the auction. This experience will benefit you greatly as you acquire it.

Chapter 4
Moving Your Treasures

Safety First

Before you start going through all of your new stuff, you need to make sure that you are safe. There are any numbers of hazards that may present themselves in your newly owned storage unit.

First make sure that your hands, which will do most of the work, are safe. It is not at all inconceivable that there will be sharp unsanitary things inside. I have seen a number of methamphetamine kits, drugs, and drug paraphernalia. I have also found plenty of used sex toys and intimate articles of clothing. Any of these items could present a health hazard from chemical or biological means.

There could also be plenty of sharp things to cut you. I have found plenty of exposed kitchen knives in boxes and broken glass. I even once bought a unit that had fifteen band saw blades. Each one of these blades was coiled up safely, except for the one that was hidden under a pile of clothes. There it lurked with plenty of razor sharp teeth just waiting to slice open an artery. I found it before there were any problems or before I was hurt, but that is not to say that I will not miss the next one.

These band saw blades could have severely cut my hands if I had not been wearing protective gloves and using a good measure of caution.

I usually wear a pair of latex gloves and a sturdy pair of leather work gloves when I am first going though a unit. In addition to protecting my hands, I also make sure that all of my body is covered. I wear pants, long sleeves and closed toed shoes as well that are suitable for heavy work. I also bring along a first aid kit to deal with any minor injuries that should arise as well. I have used this kit more than once, so make sure you have one.

Hauling Away Your Stuff

Now that you own a whole bunch of great new stuff, you need to haul it away. This can be the hardest, most physically demanding part of the job. If you are not interested in doing this yourself, there are several options that you can use.

Hire A Moving Company

If things are relatively organized, you might consider hiring a professional moving company. These people are very experienced at moving lots of heavy things. They bring all the necessary equipment with them and will get the job done in an efficient manner. The best part is that you don't have to do any of the work yourself. Instead, they will be the ones sore the next day. You need to understand that a moving company will only move organized loads in most cases. They will not organize a trashed unit for you, or if they do, will charge you heavily for this service. In most cases if there is organizing and cleaning to be done, you will need to do it yourself.

There are two types of moving companies. The first type owns and brings all of the necessary equipment with them. These are more seasoned and experienced, not to mention established companies. They will charge you a set rate that will generally include the truck and at least two movers. If you believe that more people will be needed, you can request additional people.

The other type of moving company that you may encounter does not own their trucks. Instead they load trucks that you rent. These companies are usually younger companies that are working towards expanding and buying their own truck. These companies usually charge a lower amount for the crew because you are footing the bill for a truck elsewhere. Make sure that these companies are experienced and honest. However, there is no reason that they can't get the job done for you.

Both of these companies will charge you a specific rate over a minimum period of time. In my experience, this minimum is usually three hours. Make sure that you get a quote in writing before anything is loaded on a truck.

You need to keep in mind when hiring agents to move stuff for you, that their professionalism is representative of your company. A highly unprofessional company can cause you to not be welcome back at an auction. If you do not feel this sense of professionalism from the moving company representative, you should probably choose a different company.

The easiest way to find a moving company is to use the phone book. You will need to have the specifications of the move that you are planning when calling the moving company. You will need to tell them what you have to be moved, and when you need to have it moved. You will need to give them all of your contact information, especially a phone number where you can be reached during the move. In the event of a problem you do not want movers trying to figure out what to do. This can give you a bad reputation with the business manager and the moving company.

You will also need to make arrangements to pay. Most moving companies will be reluctant to extend credit to a company that they have never dealt with. Most likely you will need to give them a credit card or pay in advance on a specified rate. You can also meet them at the job site and pay the movers directly. In the event that they do extend credit, make sure you pay them promptly and properly. As your business grows, you will have need of reliable movers, and they can sometimes be hard to find. Hold on to them once you have found them.

Temporary Labor

If you are happy loading a truck yourself but just want a little extra help over a few days, you can hire temporary labor. You can also just back the truck up to the unit you bought and have temporarily hired hands to the loading. These people work on short term contracts that are arranged by a temporary labor agency. The agency takes care of all the paperwork, payroll, and insurance headaches of hiring someone. They are the official employers of the individual people and you are "renting" them for a set amount of time. You will not pay them but will directly pay the agency that employs them. The agency will then pay the employees.

To hire people from these agencies it is best to set things up in advance. You should open an account ahead of time to make sure that everything is set up and ready to go before you need any help. When you buy a unit you will only have a few days to get things cleaned out or you will have to pay the storage company some rent. You do not want to waste any time setting up an account with a temp agency. This could cause delays that would force you to pay rent for the unit you bought and lower your profit.

Vehicles To Move Your Stuff

If you cannot move your newly bought treasures to where you can sort and sell them, there is not much point in starting a storage auction business. That being said, you will need a vehicle to do this. This will actually be your company's main asset other than its inventory so some care and diligence should go into both the decision of which type of vehicle to purchase and the actual purchasing of that vehicle.

Now, when I went out and bought my first vehicle I put a great deal of thought into that matter. I asked myself, "What is this vehicle going to do?" What I decided was that it would pick up and move merchandise, and possibly deliver the same merchandise to customers as part of a sale.

A nice big beat up van was one of the first vehicles I looked at. It would be perfect to haul anything. It had a one ton engine and about 300 cubic feet of cargo space in the back. It would be perfect to haul and engine to metal recycling, a load to the dump and a couch all at once. However, the exterior was beat up and rusted. The price was cheap and the vehicle reliable but ultimately, I decided would give a poor impression to any delivery customers.

Ultimately, I bought a minivan. I decided that its cargo space would be large enough to handle most jobs and I could always augment the hauling capacity with a trailer if I chose to. It is equally versatile in taking a load to the dump and delivering a nice kitchen table to a customer. The only trade off was I needed to pay a little more attention to keeping it clean.

Five types of vehicles are particularly useful when cleaning out a storage unit that was bought at auction. These are the step van, the pickup truck, the cargo van, the mini van and the box truck. The strengths and weaknesses of each of these vehicles are discussed in this chapter.

Step Vans

Step vans are a very common type of vehicle in commercial service fleets. They are frequently utilized by businesses that need mobile shops or service areas (like kitchens) as they can accommodate machinery and equipment and be outfitted with power systems and water supplies. Step vans offer a great deal of space for hauling around your treasures.

A typical example of a step van.

Step vans are commonly available with either gasoline of diesel engines and this can affect their fuel economy. For a 10000 gross vehicle weight (GVW) you can expect around 10 mpg for a gasoline engine and 14 mpg for a diesel engine. A truck with 10000 GVW should be sufficient for all but the largest storage units.

While step vans can be very useful to larger purchases, they may not be the ideal vehicle for a smaller operator. The large hauling capability of a step van may not be needed for small purchases. This means that the larger, more powerful engines are unnecessary and can dramatically increase the cost per mile of your vehicle.

The other downside of a step van for a smaller business is that they are more expensive than smaller vehicles. A new auction buyer would be wise to consider investing their capital in a smaller vehicle to start.

Cargo Vans

Cargo vans are vans that are smaller than step vans but larger than minivans. They offer many of the same advantages of step vans but can offer more fuel economy. The trade off is that they offer less hauling space. However, in reality the average cargo compartment is around 250 cubic feet and will offer plenty of space for moving all but the largest items.

Contemporary cargo vans are also available with gasoline or diesel engines. Both of these types of engines commonly offer around 15-20 mpg. This is a distinct improvement over a step van and with future gas prices being uncertain; this can offer significant potential savings over the life of the vehicle.

This typical example of a cargo van shows the large cargo section of this type of vehicle

The cargo capacity of cargo vans will be sufficient to haul most items. In addition to their cargo capacity, the heavy duty engines of cargo vans, when paired with a trailer, can make a very efficient system for moving even oversized pieces of furniture. Towing capacities of cargo vans range from 8000 – 10000 pounds and will easily handle a full interior and a fully loaded trailer.

Large numbers of these vans are used by craftsmen of all types and are often sold at reasonable prices when they are several years old. If well maintained these vehicles can offer many years of efficient, reliable service.

Mini Vans

Mini vans are a step down from the cargo van. These vans employ a lighter truck chassis than cargo vans and have a slightly smaller hauling capacity. Fuel economies on these vehicles are usually between 15-20 miles per gallon. These vehicles also usually come equipped with a gasoline engine. As a general rule diesel engines are hard to come by, if not impossible. Again like cargo vans, these vehicles are frequently used by tradesman because of their cargo compartments. These can also be outfitted with shelving.

While there is a smaller hauling capacity with these vans, they are very common and inexpensive. This combined with their cargo capacity and the ability to add a trailer makes them a very attractive model to consider.

Minivans make a very good storage auction business vehicle. They have hauling capacities that are big enough to tackle most moves and are commonly available at reasonable prices.

Pick Up Trucks

Pick up trucks are particularly useful to a storage auction buyer. Their open beds enable you to throw in just about anything into the bed. I have loaded up all sorts of oddly shaped and cumbersome pieces into a pickup truck bed that would have been hard to fit in a van. It is possible to use a trailer in addition to your pickup truck to haul as well.

Pickup trucks can be very useful when moving oversized and oddly shaped loads. Make sure your load is secure and stable before you start driving.

One important consideration with an open bed pickup truck is that everything needs to be tied down. Unlike with a closed van, wind while driving can easily lift and possibly cause items to go flying causing a danger to pedestrians and other motorists. Tie down straps, like those to be discussed shortly will be an absolute necessity with a pickup truck.

Pick up trucks are also commonly available in either diesel or gasoline models. The fuel economy and towing statistics of pickup trucks are similar to cargo vans.

Like the other vehicles that have been previously discussed, used pickup trucks can be easily found in most cities at reasonable prices.

Box Trucks

Box trucks are ideal for moving anything and have powerful engines, but have a low fuel economy.

Box trucks are the quintessential moving truck. They have a large hauling capacity and often have a 25000 pound gross vehicle weight rating. These trucks are very good for moving anything and often come preloaded with lift gates.

The trade off for the dramatically increased hauling capacity of these vehicles is lower miles per gallon. A truck with a 10 foot box with a gasoline engine will get around 12 mpg, while a 26 foot box truck will get between 6 – 8 mpg with either a gasoline or diesel engine.

Lift gates make loading high trucks very easy. They are a common feature on box trucks but can be added to pickups and even cargo vans.

Vehicles of this type, which fit the needs of your company, are somewhat harder to find used but by no means impossible. A great place to check is with the truck rental companies themselves. Each of these companies has to maintain a well managed and professional looking rental fleet that has no place for worn cabs and aged paint. As such, they often sell vehicles that are slightly older than they can tolerate. These trucks are still in very serviceable condition and can be had at very reasonable prices.

Trailers

Trailers can be a very useful addition to your little fleet and are worth considering. These can be used to increase the hauling capabilities of your vehicles. Additionally, open top trailers are very useful for moving oddly shaped pieces that will not necessarily fit in your truck or van.

You will need to ensure that the trailer will be suitable for your purposes before you buy it. You should determine the maximum load that it can haul by checking the trailer's weight capacity and thoroughly reading the trailer's owner's manual. You will also need to make sure that the towing package on your primary vehicle will be able to tow your trailer when it is fully loaded. Again, this information can be found in the owner's manual. One other thing that you need to be sure of is that the trailer will be able to haul its load safely. To this end you should only buy a trailer with side rails and tie down supports. This will greatly increase the safety of your trailer.

An open top trailer of this type can dramatically increase your hauling capabilities as well as help move oddly shaped pieces.

New Vs. Used. Which is right for your operation?

The question of whether to buy a new utility vehicle or a used one can be a tough question for a new business owner. When first starting out it is easy enough to convince yourself that you need the latest and greatest vehicle that money can buy. However, an important practice when just starting out is to shepherd your cash reserves and to not buy things that are not truly necessary. To that end consider the following items before buying a vehicle:

- Don't buy more vehicle than you need. Overestimating your needs can cost you big money through wasted fuel.
- Don't let vanity cost you big bucks. It is possible to convey a thoroughly professional image without buying the most expensive brand new vehicle.
- If you do decide to buy a used vehicle make sure that it is reliable by having it inspected by a professional mechanic to protect your investment.

If you decide to buy a new vehicle, finding a commercial truck dealership is very easy. Simply consult your local yellow pages. If you decide to purchase a used vehicle the following is a list of good places to look:

- Newspaper classifieds
- Online ad spaces

- Truck/Car rental companies
- Municipal auctions
- Charity auctions
- Used vehicle dealerships
- Towing companies
- Mechanics
- Other Auction Buyers

Outfitting Your Rig

Once you have decided on, and purchased a vehicle, you need to fill it with all the items you will need in the field. Below you will find a list of useful items to take with you:

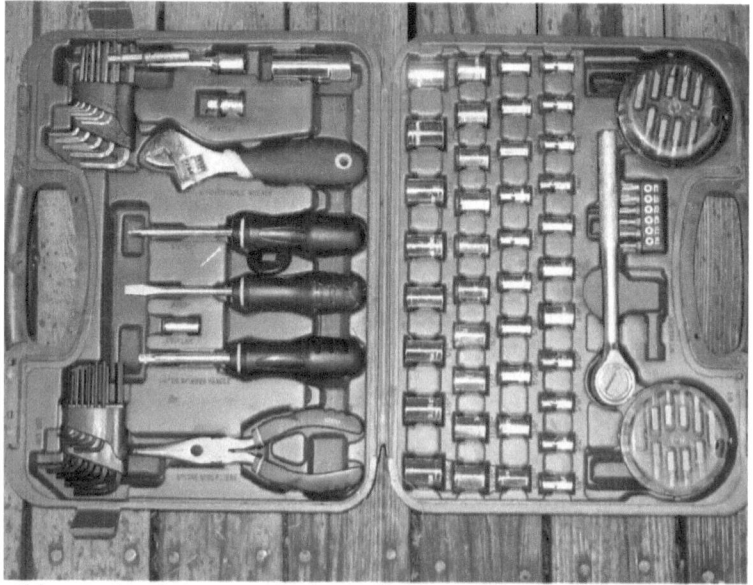

I keep this set of tools in my vehicle at all times. They have saved me more than once. I also keep a good stout mallet with me as well.

- ✓ Screwdrivers (Phillips and flathead)
- ✓ Claw Hammer
- ✓ Allen Wrenches
- ✓ Watch Screwdrivers
- ✓ Mallet
- ✓ Wrench
- ✓ Pliers
- ✓ Socket Wrench
- ✓ Level

- ✓ Electric Drill/Screwdriver
- ✓ Tape Measure
- ✓ Box knife
- ✓ Duct tape
- ✓ WD-40
- ✓ Permanent Marker
- ✓ All Purpose Cleaner in a spray bottle
- ✓ Flash light
- ✓ Batteries for the flashlight
- ✓ Paper Towels
- ✓ Garbage bags
- ✓ Tool box
- ✓ Cloth rags
- ✓ Electrical Tape
- ✓ Clipboard and clipboard rack
- ✓ Extra padlocks
- ✓ First Aid Kit (This will be handy!)
- ✓ Garbage Bags

This is merely a suggested list of items that you will find useful in your auction activities, add items as necessary.

Renting Trucks & Trailers

If you do not own a vehicle or the level of your planned activity does not make buying a vehicle worth while, you can always rent. Every type of vehicle discussed in the preceding pages can be rented. There are also no special license requirements like a commercial driver's license, unless you are driving really big trucks that are over 24' in length.

Since most of your activity will be carried out within city limits, you will always be dealing with "in city" rates. This cost is based on two charges. The first of these is a daily rental charge. This varies depending on the vehicle type you are renting, how long you will be renting it, and the demand and pricing in your area. In addition to this cost, there is a "per mile" fee as well. Again this depends on where you are and what the price of gas or diesel is doing. This charge varies over time, where the daily rental charge is fairly constant. Make sure that you know the cost per mile ahead of time.

I always buy insurance as well. A wise man once told me that the purpose of insurance was to plan for things you cannot afford. I cannot afford a $40,000 bill for a wrecked rental truck. I always make sure to read through the policy as well. These vary from company to company so I always read the fine print. Many companies do not offer insurance for damage to the box of a truck from driving somewhere too low for it. This is something you should be aware of. I also always do a walk around with the rental attendant to look for any dents or other damage to the truck. This should be part of their normal rental procedure. If they do not offer to do it, I will not rent there.

You will also need to make sure that you return the truck or van with a full fuel tank. If you do not, the company will charge you an outrageous rate per gallon to fill the tank. Make sure to hang on to that receipt as well for tax time.

Useful moving equipment

In addition to a truck to move all of your stuff, there are other tools that are needed to ensure a safe and efficient move. These items are going to be discussed in this part of the book.

All of the types of equipment discussed in the following sections are fairly inexpensive. Even so these costs may be inconvenient for a small business. That being said, most of this equipment can be purchased even cheaper by keeping an eye on the classifieds in your local newspaper. In addition all of this equipment can be rented from equipment suppliers. The cost of this is fairly reasonable as well, but can add up quickly. If you expect to be buying a lot of units, it is recommended that you seriously think about buying some used equipment to help in the process.

Hand Trucks

Hand trucks are the primary tool of the mover. They allow you to move large loads that you could not move with only your arms. They can move stacks of boxes and appliances with ease. You will need to have at least one if not several of these tools.

This hand truck can quickly be converted to a service cart. This unit has provided years of reliable service. This particular model is appropriate for small to medium loads but is unsuited for large loads like appliances.

The basic hand truck is about four feet high and has solid wheels. These types of hand trucks are used to move stacks of boxes primarily. These can be purchased at any hardware store for around $25 dollars. You can also purchase hand trucks with inflatable wheels. I have never been impressed with this design. In my experience, the tires always seem to go flat just when you need them. This makes the moving much harder. I have found solid wheels, while having a lower maximum weight rating, more reliable.

To move larger loads such as refrigerators and other appliances requires an appliance hand truck. This type of hand truck is much larger than a basic unit. These hand trucks have a higher weight rating to deal with the larger weight requirements of appliances and other large loads. Additionally, these hand trucks have included straps to secure the load while moving. Some top of the line appliance hand trucks feature a fold out set of wheels to aid with extremely heavy loads such as vending machines, or, optional automated stair climbers when no elevator is available.

Moving Carts

Sometimes, you will find that a storage unit is full of many boxes. These might not be heavy boxes and you could easily just carry them to your truck. However, sometimes you will need to negotiate hallways and elevators when moving people's stuff out and doing it one box at a time or even three at a time on a hand truck is impractical. To help overcome this you can use a moving cart.

A moving cart is a large flatbed cart that can easily be loaded with many boxes or oddly shaped pieces to quickly move them all at once.

I have used two kinds of moving carts. The first type of cart is of heavy steel construction and has a high weight capacity. These can easily be loaded with hundreds of pounds quite safely. Carts of this type are often provided free of charge by interior storage companies.

The other type of cart that I have encountered is of a lighter construction. These are made of wood, metal or plastic and have lower weight limits than the carts of all steel construction. Similarly, you can load these with many items, but pay attention to the load limits.

Moving carts can help you move large amounts of stuff with ease.

Straps

Ratcheting straps are very helpful to a mover. These are used to secure the load during transport. The ratcheting mechanism ensures a very snug fit for the load and safety for the movers.

Never under any circumstances try to move a load without first properly securing it to the vehicle with these straps. Extreme damage can result from a very heavy load (like a refrigerator) suddenly tipping over during transport. In a situation like that, property damage lawsuits may be the very least of your headaches.

No move is complete without straps to hold the load in place. Never attempt to move a load without first securing it and never exceed the maximum load rating of the straps.

Also make sure that you adhere to the maximum load rating on the straps. Never under any circumstances exceed this rating!

Clean Up After Yourself

When you buy a storage unit, you buy everything in it. Good or bad, the contents are yours. That means that it is your responsibility to remove absolutely everything in the unit. You are of course permitted to leave behind personal items.

One additional step I take is to make sure that everything is neat and tidy when I am done. Some storage companies are meticulous in requiring you to clean a unit, others are less demanding. I always clean up after myself to the best of my ability. This means that I pick up any scraps of paper that may have fallen out of boxes as I moved them. I also always sweep the unit clean before I go as well. To help with this, I always take a broom and dustpan with me when I go to auctions. You cannot count on the property providing these tools for you.

Doing all this will help lessen the workload of the manager and will be greatly appreciated. It will also guarantee that you will be welcomed back the next time that property has an auction.

The last step I take before leaving the property is to check out with the manager of the property. I tell them I am done and I invite them to check my work. Some of the managers will take you up on the offer, and others will not. This is OK. Simply offering will often be appreciated and will again convey an image of professionalism on your part.

Conclusion

Moving items after you have bought them at an auction will be the hardest part of any auction operation. I have spent many a long hot day unloading a large unit that I have bought and I confess, it is not my favorite part of this business. However, it is a necessary step before you can turn these items into cash in your bank account. Hopefully, the equipment discussions in this chapter will provide you with insight on how to more easily move your purchases.

When you are unloading, remember that safety comes first. Protect your body by wearing the right clothing and keep your eyes open for any hazards that may be present in the unit you have bought.

Chapter 5
Cashing In On Your Purchases

The whole reason that I started a storage auction business was to make money. Yes, I come across things from time to time that I buy directly from my corporation for my personal use, but most of the items that my company buys at auction are sold in order to make a profit. What this means is that you need to know how to sell your items. In this chapter, I am going to discuss some general means to sell items that you may find. After that, I will discuss particular classes of items and particulars about selling those types items. Let's dive in.

Sorting Your New Stuff

Before you can start selling your newly acquired items, and making a profit, you need to sort through and organize everything. I generally do this in my garage. However, if the unit I have bought is small, I can sort it before I move it and take everything directly where it needs to go.

My sorting process involves four categories. These are "for sale", "for donation", "for the dump", and "for recycling".

Items that fall into the "for sale" category are items that I can sell for a profit. To be in this category, the item needs to be desirable to a purchaser. I also, generally want items in this category to be ones that can be sold relatively quickly. As I have said, I do not maintain a store, so I cannot keep a large inventory. I want things coming and going all the time. If something, is in the "for sale" category, and it has not sold for a while, I will donate it to charity or let someone take it away free of charge. This allows me to free up the space and bring something else in that I can sell. This way there is a constant flow of items from auctions and cash from sales

Items that are in the "for donation" category are items that would be hard to sell quickly but that are still useful. Items that frequently fall into the "for donation" category in my operations include:

- Dishes that are not a set
- Clothes that are worn but usable
- Water glasses and coffee mugs
- Shoes
- Outdated or unattractive or scratched but usable furniture
- Holiday decorations

- Silverware

- Toys, etc.

This is really a short list. Anything that cannot be quickly sold, I will often donate to charity. This is not to say that I have not sold and made money on everyone of the items in the list above. However, I will frequently take these types of items to charity. This helps me clear out space and helps out the charities as well. Everybody is a winner. Make sure that you get a receipt for any items that you donate to charity. Keep these somewhere safe. These receipts can save you a lot of money when tax time rolls around.

Items that are "for the dump" are items that are of no use to anyone. I try to keep this category to a minimum because, to take items to the dump costs money and lowers my profit margin. However, I do take things to the dump at times. This list can include soiled mattresses, food, worn out clothing and other junk that is not recyclable.

Items that are "for recycling" are much more common than items that are for the dump. This is due to several reasons. First, it is often much better for the environment to recycle items. Also many of the items on the list that follows contain dangerous chemicals that can pose health hazards. Secondly, it is much cheaper. Most communities offer free recycling programs to encourage people to recycle rather than dump these items.

In some cases, you can even sell the items, like metal, to recyclers. Metal recyclers then sell these items to end users at a profit. Cars and car parts can be recycled as scrap metal, or you can sell them for parts. If the car or car part is a newer piece, it is worth much more as a finished part than as a piece of scrap metal.

Beyond recycling, you can also donate items for reuse to charitable organizations. The prime example that I can offer of this activity is computers. Computers are quickly outdated by newer models. A computer that may not fetch anything through resale could be of immense value to a charity. Many cities have programs that take outdated computers and refurbish them. The computers are not suited for the latest games but will run office programs and information management utilities just fine. These computers are then offered to low income and needy individuals and organizations free of charge. What is worthless to you can mean the world to someone else.

Items that I recycle include:

- Chemicals and oil
- Metal
- Cardboard (you will have a lot of boxes)
- Glass (including mirrors)
- Wood (including picture frames and furniture)
- Batteries (including car batteries)
- Auto parts
- Electronics
- Computer parts
- Paper including damaged books
- Styrofoam and packing peanuts
- Plastic

Instead of taking these items to the dump try taking them to the local recycling center. These are frequently located at the dump, but in a different area.

Taking Pictures

It is much easier to sell your newly acquired property if you take pictures of the items first. These pictures can be used in online classifieds and auctions or can be emailed to prospective customers. The old adage of a picture being worth a thousand words is definitely true in this case.

To take pictures it is really best to have a digital camera. The prices of these cameras have come done very much since they were first introduced and there is no reason that you cannot afford one these days. Watch for sales and go out and see what you can find. You should not need to spend more than $200 for a decent camera. Cameras are rated by megapixels. Cameras today go up to and beyond 12 megapixels which is well beyond the photographic capabilities of film cameras. To take photographs for my listings, I use a 4 megapixel camera that is about four years old. It is more than I need and gets the job done perfectly well.

When taking photographs I make every effort to keep it simple. These are not designed to be award winning photographs, but it is important that the pictures accurately represent what you are selling. If your picture exaggerates or misrepresents what you are selling, you will only encounter disappointed customers when folks actually come to look at and possibly purchase your item. Try and frame the item in the photograph and make sure your light is good to avoid a dark picture or one that is overexposed.

Once your photographs are taken, you may need to edit them. You can go out there and pay for state of the art photo editing software if you want. These programs can easily run into the hundreds of dollars. There is however, another option. There is a program called GIMP (GIMP stands for GNU Image Manipulation Program) that you can download for free. This program is considered open source software. These programs are maintained and developed by software programmers around the world who donate their time and expertise. I use this program to edit my photos and it has never let me down. Versions of this software are available for any type of computer platform. To download the latest version of GIMP, visit http://www.gimp.org . This software is easy to use and many tutorials are available online for the beginner or novice user.

Online Auctions

Online auctions started not long after the internet became popular. Today, some of these online auction houses have grown into companies that do billions in annual sales and conduct sales from small collectibles to enormous tracks of land to even whole cities in special cases.

No matter what type of item you have to sell, there is an online auction house that will be happy to help you sell it. The easiest way to find an auction house that is suitable to your needs, type in the item name and the word "auction" into an internet search engine. For example, to find a website that conducts auctions for classic car parts, type in "classic car parts auction" into the search field.

You do need to know a few things about online auctions before you get started. Firstly, you will need to sign up for an account with the auction house before you start listing your items. If you are operating as a corporation, make sure you sign up as a corporation to avoid any problems with commingling. Secondly, you will often need to provide a credit card number when signing up for one of these accounts. Again, make sure that you provide a company credit card and not a personal one. Your card will not be charged in most cases, but will remain on file to pay any fees that may become due.

Now, the services of an online auction house are very convenient for selling items. That being said, the service is not free. Generally, there is a fee to post your item to most online auction houses. This is called a "listing fee". Listing fees vary quite a bit and are determined by the company's policies and fee structure, the nature of the item and the listed value of the item. Additionally, many of these companies will charge a "final value fee". This is a second fee, again determined by company policy and the price of the item when it sells. You will be charged this fee upon the successful sale of the item. While these fees do vary, they are generally reasonable and are worth paying for the exposure to potential customers that these websites offer.

In addition to online auction houses, there are many financial services that have been set up to facilitate payments for online auctions with credit cards and checking accounts. Again, look for these with Internet search engines. There are additional fees for the convenience of payment that are offered by these services. Also, these services sometimes limit what items can be paid for with their services. For example, many of these services do not allow payments for firearms.

Online Classifieds

In the last few years, community specific free online classifieds have become very popular. Like, online auctions there are well known names and then there are smaller names that are no less useful when you are looking to sell something. Additionally, many local newspapers offer free online classifieds as well.

In addition to free classifieds, there are many websites out there that will allow you to post ads for specific items for a small fee. A typical example of this type of website would be a used car website. For a small fee, you can post an ad describing your car and load a picture.

I use online classifieds quite a bit to sell items. I prefer to use free ads unless the item I am selling is a high priced item that would justify paying a fee to list and ad. It is very simple. Generally, you will need to post a title and then write a short description about your item. You need to keep these descriptions very simple. State what you are selling and describe its condition. Don't get too technical, but answer any obvious questions that your customers may ask in the ad. For example, if you were listing a car, you do not need to specify the liter rating of its engine, but you should describe how the car runs and how many miles are on the odometer.

After the title and description, you will often be able to upload a picture as well. If you are taking the picture with a digital camera, take the picture on the lowest resolution setting. This will offer plenty of detail for perspective customers, but will greatly decrease the amount of time it takes for the picture to load on a web browser.

The last thing you need to consider is how prospective customers will contact you. You can post your phone number on the ad. I avoid this. The reason I do that is that, these ads are available on the internet. Unfortunately, there are programs that search through web pages looking for phone numbers and adding them to telemarketer's databases. In order to avoid this, I only list an email address (yes this does generate SPAM email). Customers can still get a hold of me this way but my phone is not ringing off the hook

Consigning Your Merchandise

Consigning your merchandise means contracting a third party to do the selling for you. This is fairly easy to do. The easiest way to consign something for sale is to find a business that already sells what you are trying to sell. Consider consignment for:

- Guns
- Used Clothing
- Furniture
- Vehicles
- Musical Instruments
- Appliances
- Computers
- Jewelry

Consigning your merchandise for sale has several advantages. First, if you are unfamiliar with selling a particular type of item, like a car. You can benefit from the sales experience of others to help fetch a higher price and faster sale than you would be able to on your own. Secondly, a store where you consign your merchandise already has an established customer base. People, who are looking for a particular item, say a trombone, know to look there. These are customers you may not be able to reach otherwise. Lastly, because you don't have to do any of the selling yourself, it is much easier to consign an item than to sell it yourself. That is the worry of the seller you have hired.

The downside to consignment is that you need to pay your seller for their service. This fee varies widely and is often dependent on the type of item you are selling and the final sales price. Before deciding to consign an item at a particular store, call around and compare their fees with other stores that accept consignments. This could save you a lot of money in fees.

Print Classifieds

Local newspapers can also be a good place to list your items for sale. In any newspaper in America, there is a section of classifieds. Many of these have a thrifty section for items under $1000 or so. Here you can place a fairly cheap, simple, "all text" ad for a few dollars.

Some of these newspapers even offer free advertising for items that are under around $500. This can extremely useful and is well worth trying. After all, what do you have to lose? If the item does not sell, it has cost you nothing and you can always relist the ad.

It is also common to find all classified newspapers in grocery stores. These can also be used to sell your merchandise, but, be aware their prices are often a little higher. I have had mixed results selling items in these newspapers over the years and would advise you to give it a try before ruling it out.

Have A Garage Sale

Americans love garage sales. They love to go to them and go bargain hunting. Just drive around Suburbia on a weekend afternoon to be convinced of this fact. This phenomenon can be very useful to you. If you have a garage full of acquisitions from auctions, or if you have purchased a very large storage unit you can consider having a garage sale.

The best items to sell at a garage sale are household items. These include but are not limited to:

- Furniture and beds
- Home appliances
- Toys and children's items
- Clothing
- Tools
- Books
- Garden equipment
- Kitchen items, dishes and silverware
- Home electronics such as TVs, DVD players and stereos

Some of these items, such as clothing and toys can be harder to sell than others and garage sales can be a great place to try your luck. Also, the only costs associated with a garage sale are your time. This can help add to your profit margin.

Some things are not appropriate to a garage sale. I always avoid selling collectibles and antiques at a garage sale. These can often be sold at a higher price and greater profit elsewhere. Also, highly technical items should not be sold through a garage sale. For example, a three axis milling machine will most likely fetch a much higher price if sold through an online auction or classified than it would through a garage sale.

Collector's Markets

Most cities have convention centers. Common occupants of these spaces are collector's markets. These go by many names really. They might be called "collector's markets", "flea markets" or "antique shows". In reality, they are often large numbers of individuals and dealers getting together to showcase their wares and sell them to the general public. These can be of tremendous value when you run a self storage auction business. They allow you, a relatively obscure person, to be exposed to literally thousands of people you would not otherwise come across. These people are at the collector's market and excited to find all kinds of treasures that they might not otherwise find in their daily travels.

Another extremely useful aspect of participating in one of these markets is the exposure to potential customers. Many of these people go to lots of these shows. They make a hobby of it in some cases. If they know who you are and what you sell, they may make a special effort to visit your tables the next time around. You can even go as far as having business cards printed up. These can list all of your contact information. If you have an online store or website, make sure that this information is on the business cards as well. With business cards that list your contact information, your customers do not have to wait until the next market to reach you. Also, if they saw something they liked and passed on it, they have a chance to change their minds.

To participate in one of these markets, you will need to purchase space. Most of the time you participate in a show by renting tables. The company that produces the show will fill the event hall with portable tables and then rent them to the merchants that plan on displaying their items. There is frequently a minimum number of tables that you will need to rent. This number is not prohibitively large in most cases. Also the fees per table are generally very reasonable as well. Remember, if you are operating as a business, these fees may qualify as a tax deductible expense during tax season.

Once you have rented tables at the show, you will arrive the day of the show before the doors open to set up. This usually requires you to be there fairly early in the morning. Set up will need to be finished by a certain time and then the doors open. You will be required to be present the whole day. There is no packing up early and leaving if you plan to be welcomed back the next time. This means it is generally a good idea to go with a partner. This will help when it is time for lunch or when you need to go to the bathroom or take a break. This person can either be a family member, or someone that you pay for their time. That decision is up to you. I have done these shows and had my wife show up for an hour to give me a break and then go home. This worked well too.

Collector's markets can be a very easy, very profitable way to sell the items that you buy in a storage auction. To find these types of markets in your area, contact your local convention center or visit their website. They profit by your participation in these markets and will be only too happy to provide you with contact information to the organizers of any upcoming events as well as a calendar listing everything that is planned in the near future.

Guns

Guns make up one of the most lucrative items that you can find inside of a storage unit. There is a high demand for this type of item and you can get high prices for many of the items that you find. If you are not familiar with guns, this section will point you to places where you can learn more.

Make sure that you pay attention to gun safety at all times. Guns can kill if handled improperly. Never take any chances. If you are unfamiliar with guns and gun safety, the National Rifle Association offers safety education courses all over the country. It would not be a bad idea to take one of these courses to make sure that you are handling guns properly when you find them. For more information, visit the NRA at www.nra.org .

Once you have safely unloaded and removed any guns that you find, you need to have them inspected by a qualified gunsmith to ensure they are safe to shoot. To find a gunsmith, you can use the yellow pages. Many websites exist that will help you with finding a gunsmith. Fees for a gunsmith's inspection vary widely. I know one gunsmith who won't even charge me even when I have tried to force the issue and I know several that charge upwards of $30.

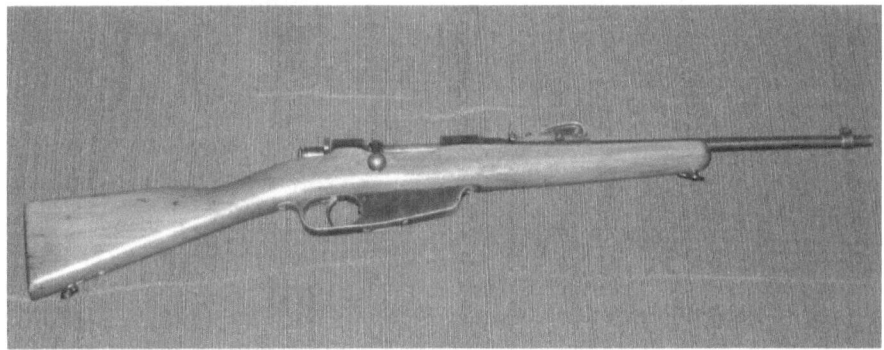

A rifle or pistol found in a purchased storage locker can turn into a large profit very quickly. Where guns are concerned, always make sure to pay attention to safety and laws governing the sale of firearms.

Before you sell any guns that you may find through your auctions, you need to identify and find out how much a gun is worth. To identify a gun first look for a manufacturer and model number. If the gun is American made, these should be stamped somewhere. Also note the serial number. These can indicate when and where the weapon was produced and greatly add to the value of the gun in some cases.

If the weapon is not of American manufacture, look for the importer's mark. This will often list the importer (you can then find their website); the caliber of ammunition that the weapon takes and the serial number that is registered with Bureau of Alcohol Tobacco and Firearms.

If the weapon is of foreign make and does not have an importer's mark, as in the case of a war trophy smuggled back into the country, you will have to do some research. Many books are available that discuss gun models in depth and these can be used to identify you gun. You can also take the gun to a gunsmith or gun dealer for help in identifying it.

There are gun price guides similar to those available for cars. These can be found online at book retailers and in electronic formats on the internet. Online gun auctions are another really good place to determine a gun's value. Find your model and see what other sellers are getting for these guns. To find these auctions (there are many online) type in "Gun Auctions" on an Internet search engine.

You can also explore what retailers are getting for these guns in used condition. Explore retailer's websites or pick up a copy of Shotgun News. Shotgun News is a magazine that explores guns and gun related subjects. Inside, you will find many pages of interesting articles as well as a very large classifieds section. There is a good chance you can find your particular gun or something close to it for a good idea of what your particular item is worth. To find a copy of Shotgun News, visit a local newsstand.

Selling guns is a little more difficult than selling other items, because the sale of guns is strictly controlled by law. There are many federal regulations concerning gun sales. To sell guns as a business, you will need a Federal Firearms License, known as an FFL. This license can be obtained from the Bureau of Alcohol Tobacco and Firearms at www.atf.gov .

Another option for selling guns is to consign them to a licensed dealer for sale. This means that you do not have to obtain an FFL or pay the fee. Also, complying with all the laws of a sale becomes the responsibility of the licensed dealer. Additionally, a licensed dealer who deals in guns exclusively will have a better understanding of the market and most likely will be able to sell the gun at a higher price and more quickly. Now, there is a trade off. To consign a gun for sale, you will give up some of your profit as a fee to the dealer. This is the method that I prefer to use as an FFL can take several months to obtain and costs a $200 fee.

Your last option for making money from a firearm is to sell it to a dealer or a pawn shop directly. These stores will give you cash that day and the sale is done. The downside to this arrangement is that pawnshops will generally offer you a much lower amount of money compared to direct sale or consignment. They will require you to present identification. If you are operating your business as corporation make sure that any paperwork, such as a receipt is made out in the name of your business.

Tools

Tools are a great item to find in storage auction. Everybody needs tools and tools wear out and need to be replaced. Also, new quality tools can be very expensive. All this means that tools bought in an auction can be a great profit source for your business.

There are two types of tools that you will encounter. The first type of tools, are well made brand name American manufactured tools. These tools have excellent reputations for quality and are sought after by professionals who make their livings from tool use such as contractors and mechanics because of their reliability and quality.

The second types of tools that you will encounter are tools designed for non-commercial use. These tools are usually imported tools and are less expensive to buy. These tools are well suited for home use and are not intended for rigorous prolonged use. These are the types of tools I keep in my vehicle and they have served me well in a number of cases.

I have bought and sold both of these types of tools. Either one is easy to sell and make money from. Well known, name brand tools, I will generally sell through online local classifieds, the free sections of my local newspaper, or pawn shops. I will take the item to a pawnshop last, again, because they often offer the lowest price. Also, if you know any contractors, mechanics, or tradesman who make use of the tool type you are selling don't hesitate to mention it to them. You could have a sale in no time.

The tools intended for home use are often harder to sell on their own. This is not because they are poorly made or unreliable, but because they are generally lower cost items. Say you find a nice imported ratchet set in a unit. This set is in great condition and has all the parts and looks unused. Well, this particular ratchet set can be bought for $15 at stores all over town. As a rule, I try to sell my tools for around 50% of the cost of a new one. This means that I can really only hope to get $7.50 for this ratchet set. Who is going to spend all day driving across town, to buy a used ratchet set, when they can drive a few minutes from their house and buy a new one for $15. If you take into account gas, then the cost to them for the new and used tool set is the same.

Grouping tools together and selling them as a lot can be an easy way to sell them.

So, what I like to do with non-commercial tools like this is assemble them in a package. I will not try to sell one hammer, or one wrench, but instead will wait until I have a good set of household tools and sell them as a lot. This makes the items easier to sell, because customers are getting a good enough deal to make it worth their time to come over and pick them up.

In addition to tools, I have encountered apartment sized ladders, workbenches, and vices as well. I threw all of those together with a large set of tools and sold them as an "apartment workshop". That bundle went really quickly. Someone got some nice tools and I profited from items that would have been hard to sell on their own.

If you happen to buy a lot of tools that have been poorly cared for and are corroded and rusted, or are in poor working order otherwise, you can always sell them as scrap. This should be a last resort because this option will give you very little return, if any, on your original investment.

Scrap Metal

The last several years has seen a dramatic increase in the price of many metals. There are several factors that have created this situation. First, increases in oil and other fuels have made refining ore from the ground into finished metals much more expensive. Also, economic expansions by countries like India and China have greatly increased the demand for many metals as well. All of this has driven the price skyward and in a hurry.

This situation has created another side effect. There is a great demand for recycled metals. These are often less costly than extracting more metals from the earth. Many companies that operate metal recycling businesses have posted record sales and profits lately as well due to this fact.

This can be of great benefit to you. Companies that refine and sell recycled metals in large quantities buy metal from small companies and individuals. They often pay very good prices for metal items that are of no more use than as scrap metal.

One time, I was at an auction. It was a piece out auction, so everything was being sold off item by item. The unit that was being sold looked like a cable installer. There were lots of cable boxes, computers, and most relevant, spools of wire. Nobody seemed interested in the wire. So I offered a bid of $2 per spool. This bid was almost an insult, but I won! I wound up buying a total of six spools. They were a mix of coaxial cable (used for cable hookups), telephone wire, and CAT5 cable (used for high speed internet). I loaded these into my car and headed to the metal recycler.

Spools of wire like this one contain valuable amounts of recyclable copper.

Copper is one of the most sought after of non-precious metals and commands a high price. I knew that the wire that I had bought was pure copper with a little insulation on it. I wound up selling it for $87. With my $12 investment, this was a more than 700% profit in less than an hour.

This story illustrates how wonderful profits can be made from scrap metal and why you should pay attention to any metal you find in a unit.

The four types of metals that can easily be sold to metal recyclers are copper, brass, aluminum and iron (this includes all types of steel). You do not have to be an expert to sort these four types of metals. Copper, solid brass and aluminum will not be attracted to a magnet. This fact makes a magnet an essential tool when sorting metals.

Copper is the color of pennies and is often used for electrical wires and plumbing fixtures. If you suspect that you are dealing with a piece of copper, run a magnet over it first. If the magnet is not attracted to it, chances are you are dealing with pure copper. If the piece is copper colored and is attracted to a magnet, you are most likely dealing with copper covered steel.

Brass is a mixture of copper and zinc. This type of metal is a dull yellow and is often used for bullet casings. Brass is also often used as accents on doors and furniture. Brass is also not attracted to a magnet in its pure form. If the magnet is attracted to a piece that you think is pure brass, again, it is most likely steel plated with brass.

Aluminum is a silver colored metal. If you have ever used aluminum foil, often called "tin foil", or drank out of a soda can, you are familiar with Aluminum. Aluminum has many uses. It is used in aircraft, wiring, electrical components, computer cases, hard drives, cooling fans and many other applications. Aluminum is not attracted to a magnet and is easily distinguished from copper and brass by its color. Use the magnet test to separate steel from Aluminum.

Iron or steel are very common metals. Without a doubt, modern society would grind to a halt without iron and steel. It is used everywhere. As a result of its high availability, these metals will fetch the lowest price as scrap. Iron and steel are easy to spot because of their attraction to a magnet. Stainless steel will also fall into this category.

Find a metal recycler in your area by consulting the phone book. You can also contact your city's garbage transfer station. They will be able to point you to a metal recycler in your area.

Recyclers will often give you a choice of being paid in cash or with a check. I prefer to have a check. This creates more documentation, which in business can always be helpful. Also, with a check, you can have the recycler issue the check directly to your business. Again, as with guns, you will need to show identification. This may seem odd, but with the high price of metals, many thieves have taken to stealing metal for scrap to make a quick buck.

Gold and Silver

There is nothing quite as exciting as finding jewelry in a storage locker. Finding some gold and silver is not only possible, it happens pretty frequently. When I find an item that I think is either gold or silver, the first thing I do is look for a marking confirming it.

Pure gold is unsuitable for jewelry, so it is often mixed with other metals to form an alloy. The gold content is measured in the form of karats. Pure gold is 24 karats. In the United States, most gold jewelry is 10, 14 or 18 karat. Countries on the Persian Gulf often produce gold jewelry at 22 karats. European gold jewelry is marked with the percentage of gold in thousandths. For example, 14k or 58.5% gold will be marked as 585. 18 karat gold will be marked as 750, and so on.

You need to look out for gold filled and plated pieces as well. These jewelry items are made of a base metal (usually a steel alloy) and are then covered with gold to a varying thickness. These pieces of gold are usually marked with symbols like "G.F." "Gold Filled" or "10k, 14k, 18k or 24k H.G.E" (High Gold Enamel).

Silver is not divided into a karat system like gold. Silver employs the European system of listing the percentage of silver in thousandths. Sterling silver, which is mostly silver with a little hardener, will be marked "925". Lower quality silver alloys will be marked in a similar style but with a lower rating.

Usually an item that is marked with one or more of the symbols described above, will be gold or silver. However, if you are still unsure, there are electronic testers and chemical kits that you can buy for further analysis. These tools and kits are a little expensive and in the case of a chemical test, can be damaging to the jewelry if used improperly. You can also always seek the opinion of a jeweler. Most of the jewelers I have met are happy to offer their help and opinions, often free of charge.

A small digital scale that weighs items in ounces, grams, troy ounces, and pennyweights is a very useful tool when dealing with jewelry and precious metals.

After, you have determined that what you have is gold or silver you should weigh it to determine just how much it is worth. To weigh my jewelry, I have a small pocket scale that I purchased at a local hardware shop. The scale I have measures weight in ounces, grams, pennyweights and troy ounces. Troy ounces and pennyweights are the preferred units of measurement for precious metals. When gold and silver prices are quoted in the newspaper, they are quoted for a troy ounce. A pennyweight is $1/20^{th}$ of a troy ounce.

To figure out the value of your gold or silver, weigh it in troy ounces. Then multiply that number by the percentage of metal in the piece as determined from the markings on the item. Lastly, multiply that number by the price of gold or silver that day. A formula would be:

Weight in Troy Oz. x Percent of Pure Metal x Price per Troy Ounce

For example, say you have a 14k gold ring that is $1/10^{th}$ of a troy ounce, and gold is worth $750 per troy ounce. So the value of the piece would be found by:

(.1 Troy Ounces) x (14k/24k) x ($750 per ounce) = $43.75

To make money on gold and silver jewelry, you have several options. The first is to sell the item yourself to a customer who plans to use the jewelry. Next, you can sell the jewelry to another retailer and be done with it. Along a similar line, you can consign the jewelry to another retailer to sell it for you. Lastly, you can sell the metal for scrap.

To sell jewelry directly to the end user, I use an online auction or a classified ad. I prefer online auctions because you do not have to go meet the person who is buying the item. This may seem odd, but, it is really not my favorite thing in the world to go and meet a person with a very valuable item for which I must insist they pay cash. This creates a robbery potential. If you are going to meet someone, make sure that you adhere to certain common sense safety standards. Meet somewhere in public and if something feels odd, just pass on the meeting.

I do not like trying to sell jewelry to other jewelers. They try to offer you the lowest price they can, and often I do not care for the process. However, this is definitely an option that you can choose. If you live in a major city, I am sure you can find a jeweler that buys silver and gold. Take them what you have and see what they offer you. One thing I would recommend is to know the approximate retail price of the jewelry before walking into anyone's shop. If they think you do not know what you are talking about, they may try to take advantage of you. If you like their price, take it and be done. If you do not like the price they offer you, ask them if they would be willing to consign the piece or pieces. The worst they can do is say no.

Lastly, you can sell your gold and silver as scrap. This works in much the same way that recycling copper, brass, aluminum or steel works except that the prices are higher and the weights are much lower. Around the country are metal refineries that deal exclusively in precious metals. They refine the metals to varying standards and sell them to other industries as raw metal. As for gold, they produce ingots that are sold to jewelers, electronics manufacturers, dentists, etc. Similar industries need silver as well. Instead of extracting the metal from the earth, these companies buy metals at a slight discount and then melt them down. For example, a piece of gold jewelry that was made in 1974 and is just hideous, could find its way into several beautiful new creations through a precious metal recycler.

To find a precious metal refiner in your area, use the Internet. These companies can be spread out all over the country and a local one is preferable. I know I don't like sending $1000 worth of gold in the mail. On that note, you should pay attention to two points. First, if you are going to use a precious metal recycler, make sure it is a company that is well known and is trustworthy. You can start small and if you are happy, increase your shipments. Secondly, if you do send packages of precious metals in the mail, make sure that you have a receipt for them and strongly consider buying insurance to protect your shipment from loss.

Furniture

Furniture is one of the most common items that people store at mini storage parks. It makes sense if you think about it. Furniture is large and takes up a lot of space that many people just don't have. Also, furniture can be expensive, so while many people may not have room for it at present, it can be worth paying rent if they plan to use it in the future when they move into a bigger home.

I personally love buying furniture in a storage auction. Usually, if the furniture turns out to be in decent condition, you can recoup your purchase price from just a few pieces and make a healthy profit from just a few more. Also, furniture is generally easy to sell. People are always in need of furniture. Also, no matter what type of furniture you have, someone is in the market for it. College kids on their own for the first time are often less discriminating than older more established customers and will buy older less stylish furniture. The price of course will reflect this. If you have top quality antique furniture, there are plenty of folks who would love to add its charm to their home as well. Again, the price will reflect this.

The first thing that you need to do when you have a piece of furniture is to clean it up. A lot of the time, these pieces will get dirty and dusty in storage. This layer of grime will make it harder to identify your piece and harder to sell it.

Before you attempt to clean anything, you need to make sure that you will not damage the furniture. Only furniture with a "hard finish" like varnish, shellac or lacquer should be cleaned with chemicals like mineral spirits or soap. Oil finishes should never be cleaned with chemicals, as it will damage the finish. For cleaning oil finished furniture, seek professional advice.

This bed frame was originally covered with candle wax and soda residue. After cleaning and polishing it can add charm to any bedroom.

To determine if the piece has a hard or oil finish, apply some mineral spirits to a bathroom cotton swap. Apply this swab somewhere inconspicuous on the item and see if the finish softens. If the finish does soften, the finish is oil. If the finish remains the same it is a hard finish.

Once I have made sure that the finish will be safe, I use three basic chemicals to clean my furniture. These chemicals are mineral spirits, Ivory Bar™ soap, and Old English™ furniture polish. I prefer Ivory Bar™ soap, because it does not leave any residue like detergents can and offers a good gentle cleaning power. Mineral spirits are useful for removing things like candle residue or any adhesives or tars. I use the Old English™ to give a healthy glow to the piece I am cleaning. Also, polishing helps gloss over any little imperfections that may be in the finish and can quickly restore the piece to exquisite condition.

You may be very surprised to see what you have once you have cleaned your furniture. I once bought a unit that had a dresser in it. This dresser was unpretentious and did not look like anything special. It was a little beat up as well. Once I had cleaned it and taken out the contact paper from the drawers, it turned out that it was made out of mahogany. This made it a valuable find and I made a nice profit off of it.

The next step before selling your furniture is to price it adequately. Again, this is very subjective. If I am unfamiliar with an item or uncertain of its value, I find similar new and used pieces and base my price on those numbers. Some especially valuable pieces may be worth employing an appraiser to do the work for you. If you have a Louis XIV chair, trust me, an appraiser will be well worth his fee!

To sell furniture, you can use any of the techniques previously discussed. I personally prefer direct sale through the classifieds or consignment if the pieces are nice enough. One additional consideration with furniture sales is that many people will not have vehicles large enough to move furniture. What will your policy be on that? Do you make them rent a truck and do it themselves? This may turn a lot of potential customers into people who pass. Maybe you can go and deliver the items in your truck, if you have one that is. This would have the effect of burning a lot of your gas. Do you charge a fee for that? These are some questions to ask yourself. I have done deliveries, people have shown up with trucks, and people have rented trucks before ever showing up to look at the furniture. All of these methods are fine; just know how far you are willing to go to make a sale in advance.

Collectibles

The term collectible can be a hard one to pin down and can mean many things to many people. Really, it just means anything that is collected. This can mean lots of things such as toy cars, porcelain dolls, salt and pepper shakers, coins, stamps, glassware, knives, sports cards, sports memorabilia, beer memorabilia, non-sports trading cards, war memorabilia, newspapers from famous days, etc.

These can all be very valuable finds when you come across them after an auction. In many cases, you will find whole collections. At that point you will need to decide if you are going to sell off the whole collection or each piece separately. Selling the whole collection is a way to get a good price right away, however, selling each piece on its on can take longer but often make more money if the pieces are rare enough.

Even a small collection of toy cars like this one, can fetch a surprisingly high price.

To determine what prices are appropriate for collectibles, there are many different price guides available. Depending on what you have found, you may be able to find online websites that will list current prices, or you can visit a local library or bookstore. These price guides often have chapters in the beginning of them, explaining the items they cover. Always read these if they are present. They will expand your knowledge of the item type for use in the future and will help you learn how to use the guide itself.

Some collectibles are so popular that stores may exist in your area that deals in them specifically. An example of this would be sports cards. If you are looking to make a quick sale (sometimes a fast nickel is better than a slow dime) you can take your collection to a store like this and see if they are interested in buying it from you. If your price expectation is reasonable this can be a great way to sell any collection that you find.

This collection of sports cards had 10 years worth of basketball, football, and baseball cards, including many valuable ones. This was a very profitable sale.

Musical Instruments

Musical instruments are another potentially lucrative find inside a purchased storage locker. Realistically, you are not going to find a 17th Century handcrafted Italian violin, but I have encountered many very nice electric guitars, brass instruments and drums. In addition to the instruments themselves, you may also encounter useful amplifiers.

It is very important that you do your homework when pricing musical instruments. The tastes of musicians are very fickle and small subtle differences in instruments can make a huge difference in both the demand for the instrument and the price. Also, the quality of the item is something to which you need to pay very close attention. For example, quality of the cork connectors on certain woodwind instruments like clarinets needs to be in good condition. If the cork is bad it will need to be replaced. This can easily cost as much as a new instrument. With specialty items like instruments, again as with guns, the trained eye of a professional can be of enormous help in determining the quality and value of the item. As with most of the other items described in this chapter, price guides are available to help you with pricing the item.

Selling musical instruments is fairly easy as well. I will generally place classified ads or use online auctions to do the selling. You can also take the items to a musical instrument or pawn shop and see what they would give you for the item. Again, as they will most likely resell it anyway and need to make a profit, they will offer you a lower price than you could command by selling it to an end user.

One interesting phenomenon with musical instruments is that there is often a greatly increased demand for instruments in the fall and a slackening during the spring and summer months. Often, you will find prices are higher in the fall and lower in the summer as well. Believe it or not, this is due to school children. Think about it. When school starts in the fall each year all the children participating in musical programs need instruments. So the parents go out and buy an instrument for their child. This is what causes the increase in demand and pricing. When school ends, often you will find parents selling the instruments to recoup their money. This causes a decrease in demand and a corresponding drop in price. This is something to consider when selling any instruments. As with all things, timing can be everything.

Clothing

People store lots of clothing in storage complexes. You will encounter huge piles of clothing if you choose to start a storage salvage business or hobby. Be ready for it. Many auction buyers look at clothing as a liability. I however, do not, and have made very healthy profits off clothing since I started going to auctions.

The first thing you need to do is make sure that the clothing is clean. This is essential. Unfortunately, not all off the clothing that goes into storage is going to be clean. I will often use my washer and dryer to get things clean. If you are concerned about damaging your personal appliances, or have an abnormally large amount of clothes, you can always go to a laundromat and use their industrial sized machines.

Once everything is clean, I sort the clothes into piles based on whether the clothing is men's, women's, or children's clothing. As I am sorting, I look over each article to see if it has any stains, cuts or holes. If it does, I immediately add it to any pile for donation that I have. I also look to see if the clothing is contemporary and is still appropriate to wear. If it is, it goes on its respective pile. If the clothing is more of a "period" piece and could be considered "retro", set it aside for special consideration. Retro clothing can often be worth a small fortune to the boutique shops that deal exclusively in this type of clothing. A trip to one or several of these boutiques can really be worth your time.

To sell my clothing, I prefer selling to second hand clothing stores, consignment, or direct sales through online auctions. These are really the easiest ways to unload your inventory. You can use internet and print classifieds if you have a very special item, or an item that is worth a fair amount of money, say for example, a brand new three piece suit. This sort of valuable item may get enough attention and there may be enough desire to warrant someone coming to pick it up. However, the majority, of clothing will not be valuable enough to make use of classifieds.

Selling to second hand clothing stores or consigning clothing is fairly straightforward. However, there are several tips that can make selling your clothing with online auctions much easier. I will often set prices, very low. Usually, I will use a base price of $.99. This gives people the impression that they are receiving a deal and this often encourages people to bid on your auction. In reality, they are getting a deal; however, because of the prices you paid at auction you are still making a good profit. In the used clothing stores where I live, a polo shirt will often cost between $5 and $7. Buying one for $.99 at an online auction could be a real steal.

I also always include pictures of the actual item that I am selling in the auction. You can do this several ways. You can photograph the item in a nice folded state, unfolded and lying on something, or on a mannequin. This last option is the one that I prefer. This gives customers the ability to see how the item hangs. Since customers are not able to touch and feel, or try on a garment that is being sold over the internet, this makes a sale much more likely. Mannequins can often be found used for $50 or less. This is not a bad investment if you plan on selling a fair amount of clothing and is a piece of equipment that I would recommend purchasing.

Computers

I frequently find computers in the units that I buy. They are common and often find their way into storage. I am also a bit of a computer nerd, so I do enjoy finding computers and tinkering with them.

You might think selling a computer is a fairly straightforward proposition, however, there are a number of points that you should consider first.

The first thing you need to do is make sure that the computer is indeed in working order. Storage lockers sometimes suffer water leakage and this can ruin a computer that was put into storage in working order, or it may have been broken when it was placed in storage. Either way, the easiest way to determine if it is in working order, is to plug it in and power it up. If it powers up and starts displaying messages on the monitor, chances are you are in good shape.

You also should be concerned with the software on the computer. There is not guarantee what so ever, that the software on the computer is legal software. As such, I never leave this on any computer that I sell. Selling software that has been illegally copied can land you in hot water and this is definitely something you want to avoid. Also, unless you have looked at every file on a computer, you cannot be certain that things such as child pornography are not on the computer. To eliminate all of the possible headaches and make sure that whatever I am selling is legal, I always format all hard drives in any computer I buy before selling it. To find information on formatting a hard drive, do a quick internet search. There are many free programs that you can download that will do this for you.

At this point, you need to decide if you are selling the computer without any software. If you are going to sell the computer without any, simply move ahead with any of the selling techniques so far described in this book. Make sure that you know the model number of the computer. With this, you can get all the specifics online. If you do want to sell the computer with software, and you feel comfortable loading an operating system onto a computer, you can download any one of the free versions of Linux.

Linux is a very robust, complete and free operating system that is put together and maintained by software engineers around the world who donate their time and expertise. The software can be freely downloaded and installed on any computer for free without any worrying about licensing. This allows you to load the computer with a useful set of programs without any worrying about licensing. This also increases the perceived value of the item and can help add to your profit. To find a distribution of Linux that is current, search for Linux on an Internet search engine.

An added sales technique that you can take advantage of with computers is selling the parts individually. You can often take a computer that is a little past its prime, disassemble it to its base parts, and sell the parts for more than you could have sold the whole system. This is similar to the business model that junkyards use when selling car parts. Whatever is left over can be donated to computer recyclers, or if it is metal, sold for scrap.

There are six parts that you should pay special attention to when selling a computer for parts. Theses are:

- The motherboard
- The hard drive(s)
- RAM
- CD/DVD drive and burners
- The processor
- The case

The motherboard is the main system board of the computer. All other parts plug into this piece and it also houses the processor. Motherboards can be very competitive and are specific to the processor that they can hold. To identify a motherboard, look for the manufacturer's name and a serial number. This information can be entered into a search engine to help identify the trade name and particulars of the motherboard that you have.

The hard drive is the magnetic storage device of the computer and holds all programs. Hard drives can be worth a pretty penny depending on the size of the hard drive and the amount of programs and files that it can hold. Again, look for a manufacturer's name and serial number to identify the part that you have.

The RAM on a computer is the main system memory and determines the speed that the computer can execute a program. There are several types of RAM, so make sure that you know which one you have before advertising it. You can find guides describing RAM types online. RAM is measured in terms of clock speed and capacity. The clock speed is given by number similar to "PC3200" and the capacity is by a rating similar to "512 MB" or "1 GB". You will need all this information to describe the RAM properly in any ads.

DVD burners are the most sought after disk drive these days. However, old fashioned CD-ROMs and CD burners will also fetch you a nice return on your investment. Identify and sell these, again using any manufacturer's name and serial number information that you can retrieve.

Any processors that you find in a computer can be a very good find. These are small and easily sold through the mail. To remove the processor from the computer, look for a small release latch on the motherboard. This will free the processor. Processors in computers are often coated with a thermally conducting grease to protect the processor from heat. To remove this, use a little rubbing alcohol. This will allow you to see the manufacturer's information and identify the processor model.

The case is the last major part of the computer that can be sold at a profit. The basic case is called an ATX case. This means that the computer parts have standard layouts that are guaranteed to fit inside the case. Cases are bulkier items and I prefer to sell them locally if I can. If I get a bunch of these in my inventory, I can always take them to a metal recycler.

The biggest market for selling computer parts is through online auctions on well known websites. Many people are out there looking for these parts and you can often make very quick and profitable sales.

Consumer Electronics

Electronics are another highly desirable class of items to find in your auction winnings. Televisions and stereos are probably the easiest items to sell and make a pile of money on, but this category also includes DVD players, digital cameras, speakers, and VCRs. These items are usually quick movers and I buy them whenever I get the chance at an auction.

The first step you need to take when inventorying any consumer electronics you find is to make sure that they work, and work properly. To do this, I keep a workspace in the garage that is hooked up with a powers supply, a small TV, some speakers, a VCR, a DVD player and some DVDs and CDs. This is a basic electronics test bench. First, I plug in whatever I have bought and make sure that it powers on. If it does, we are in business. If the unit does not power up, after checking to make sure that my power supply is good, I look for any problems with the power cord of the device. Sometimes the connection is loose and needs to be reattached. I have even bought a television where the power cord had been chewed through by what looked like a puppy. This was interrupting the supply of electricity to the TV. To fix this, I cut off the damaged part of the cord and attached a new plug to the shortened cable. The TV worked fine after this and it is in my living room as I write this.

This television had a cord that had been chewed through. A quick replacement plug from a hardware store was all that was needed to make this item a quick profitable sale.

After you decide that the device you are testing powers on, you need to test the quality of the item's performance. This is important.

An item can power up, but still perform well below accepted levels. Selling an item like this as an item in good working order will result in a very angry customer and will not generate any sales leads or recommendations in the future. To make sure that the item's quality is appropriate, I always put it through its paces before selling it. For a television, I will hook the TV up to cable, a DVD player and a VCR and watch the screen. I look to make sure that the picture quality for all three inputs is good. Some televisions that I have bought looked great, but upon more careful inspection, revealed that they had poor picture and sound quality, or were missing common inputs like RCA plugs. These facts made the TVs less than sellable and they were donated.

To test a DVD player, I keep a few DVDs that I do not care about with my test bench. Actually, the DVDs were bought at a storage auction too. I hook the player up to a small TV that I keep in the garage and watch some DVDs on it. I look for any problems like skipping, scratchy picture or dialog not matching the picture. If any of these problems occur, after cleaning the device, I will not sell the DVD player. The process for testing a VCR is very similar.

To test any stereo equipment that I find, I will hook up the system, either with its own speakers, or speakers I provide and run the stereo through some hurdles. First, I test to see if it plays CDs and that their sound quality is good. Next I will tune in several radio stations to make sure that the radio tuner is in good condition and easily fixes on a signal. If all of this is in good shape, I will give the stereo a clean bill of health and can then sell it.

Digital cameras are slightly different from TVs, DVDs, VCRs, and stereos, in that they are a still quickly evolving technology. What I mean by this is simple. TVs are fairly straightforward. New bigger models and HD models are appearing but, they all perform the same basic function. This is not true with digital cameras. The photo quality on the latest model of digital camera is constantly increasing at the same time the size of the devices are rapidly shrinking, as is the price of the latest model. When I find a digital camera, I always try and sell it as quickly as possible to combat these effects. Also, if it is a few years old, you might not get a very good price for it because it has been replaced by a newer sleeker model.

Household Items

Household items are anything that can be used in the home that does not fall into other popular categories such as electronics. This includes many things that you will certainly find including, but not limited to:

- Dishes and glasses
- Pots and pans
- Kitchen utensils
- Small appliances such as microwaves and coffee makers
- Wall art
- Space heaters and air filters

This is really a small list and is by no means exhaustive. These items are generally small, common items that are not worth a lot of money on their own and you will be hard pressed to sell in the classifieds or even with online auctions. Most of the items that fall into this category would make excellent inventory for a garage sale or swap meet. In one of these settings, these items could be quickly and easily sold for the lower prices that dominate at these events.

It is not uncommon to encounter very large amounts of these types of items in a single unit. More than once, I have bought a unit and found the entire contents of someone's kitchen, packed safely in many boxes. Think about that for a second. How much is there in your kitchen? How many boxes would that fill? I will tell you, it is a lot. Often, you will find complete, unopened sets of dishes, glasses, pots, pans, silverware, baking equipment, etc.

In a situation like this, I like to sell the whole set as a complete kitchen. This can make selling the items much easier. When I first moved out of my parent's home, I had nothing in the way of kitchen equipment. Buying a whole kitchen at a fair price like this would have interested me very much. Once, when I was selling a unit like this, I was contacted by a woman who had suffered a house fire. They had lost all of their kitchen gear and were in need of everything that I had for sale. I empathized with her and gave her a good price. It was a win for both of us. She replaced ten years worth of kitchen tools in an afternoon and I still made money on the deal.

Instead of selling all of these items for $1 a piece over several weeks, these items were marketed as a lot for $50. They sold in one afternoon.

Some items, like microwave, toaster ovens, and bread makers will command a high enough price that you can sell them through online, local ads or online auctions. This is my preferred method for dealing with items like this. A general rule that I follow is, that if the replacement cost of an item is more than $50, I can sell it through an online classified or auction. Any lower than that, and I can sell it at my next garage sale, or package it with other like items for a lot sale.

Books

I love finding books in a unit that I have bought. I won't lie. I love going through books. Books can also be a very valuable find, depending on what you find and how you sell them.

Most of the time, books that you find in a storage locker will be commonplace paperbacks that do not have any special value. These can still be worth money at a used bookstore. However, every now and again, you can make a very valuable find. For example, a complete set of 19th century classic literature will be worth a handsome sum.

Before you start selling your books, you should know exactly what you have to offer. This means that you need to identify your books. Most modern books carry a unique identifying number called and ISBN. This stands for "International Standard Book Number". This number comes in two forms. The first form is known as an

ISBN-10 and the second is ISBN-13. As a result of the ever increasing number of books that are published, the international book community recently expanded the number of digits in an ISBN number from 10 to 13. This adds many more numbers that can be used for books that are published in the future. Most books in print today carry and older ISBN-10 10 digit number. Only books that have recently published now carry a 13 digit ISBN-13. You will also commonly find both forms of the ISBN on one books.

To find the ISBN of any book, you only need to look in three places. The first place to look is the back cover of the book. Often the number will be listed in one of the bottom corners. If the book has a barcode on the back, the ISBN will be listed above the barcode image. Usually, it will be preceded by the word "ISBN". If, there is no barcode on the back cover, or the ISBN is not listed on the back, you can try looking on the inside of cover or on the dust jacket. Sometimes there will be a barcode and ISBN printed there. The last place to look and one that is almost guaranteed to contain the ISBN is the copyright page. This page is located immediately after the title page.

Once you have found the ISBN, you can find the title information and price of the book using an online book retailer or an Internet search engine. Most online book retailers will allow you to search their catalog with the ISBN number. If you are using an Internet search engine, type in the phrase "ISBN" before the number so the search engine knows what kind of number it is looking for. Any webpages that are returned will be the exact same title and edition that you have in your possession. If the retailer sells only new books, you can see what a new copy is priced for and from that determine how much you can sell the book for. If the retailer sells used books as well, you can immediately see the state of the market for that particular book from the amount of people that are selling the work. Prices can be found by seeing how much they are selling for.

To sell and make money from books, you have two options. The first is to take them to a local used book store and sell them directly to the store. This is often a great option. They take the books off of your hands that day and then they deal with the headache of selling and shipping the books. Now, because you are doing less of the work yourself, you can expect a lower price for the books you are selling. Another option that many used booksellers offer is a higher trade in value for books. This means that they will offer you two prices. One is the amount of cash they will give you for your books. The other price they will quote you is the value of house credit they will offer you for the books. They trade in value is generally higher. This can be great if, like me, you are an avid reader and are constantly in need of new books to fill your shelves. Trading the books in and using the credit yourself, may be a problem if you are operating as a corporation. You may need to sell the books from your corporation to yourself before you sell them to the bookstore. If you are uncertain, discuss this with a qualified attorney.

To fetch a higher price on your books, you can sell them directly in any one of the many online book marketplaces. This is a very easy alternative to selling the books to a book retailer. It is also attractive in that you do not have to find the customers. The retailer takes care of that. You simply offer your used book inventory as part of the retailer's inventory. In most cases, you will need to sign up for an account first. This is easy to do and only takes a few minutes. Often, you will be asked for bank account information as well. Do not be alarmed. This is simply so the company can pay you what is owed to you using electronic transfer directly to your account.

Once the account is all set up, you will begin selling your books. Most of these retailers have simple forms for you to fill out that will include your item in their inventory. You will need to fill in the ISBN, the condition of the book, and your price, and that is about all. When the books sell, you will receive an email letting you know that you need to ship. Make sure that you send "media mail" unless the customer has paid for a more expensive service or you will spend all of your profits in shipping.

If you find lots of books and are doing a lot of selling, see if the retailer you use offers a volume selling service. These have lower listing fees, but an added monthly service fee. Often you will be given access to volume selling tools as well as detailed sales statistics. If you are selling mountains of books, it might be worth your time and money to sign up for one of these services as they can be cheaper.

Mattresses

Mattresses are one of the most common items that I find in storage units. I have bought some units that were nothing but mattresses. In one unit there must have been no less than 15 complete bed and box spring sets. Mattresses can be a valuable find. In some cases, these days, quality mattresses can cost over $2000 brand new and will fetch a good price in the used market. Mattresses can also be a real headache. Of the 15 bed sets that I found in that one storage unit, seven of them must have been soaked with cat urine. Just try selling those or any of the ones in storage with them! The only thing that you can do in that case is truck them to the local garbage dump. This can result in a steep dumping charge and absolutely no profit.

Because of the stains on this mattress, the only choices for getting rid of it were giving it away and taking it to the dump. It was given away to avoid a dump fee.

I also know sellers who will burn mattresses instead of taking them to the dump. This could be an option for you. If you choose to take this option, check with your local department of environmental quality to determine when and how you can burn items in your area.

If you are fortunate enough to find a mattress that is in good condition and can be sold, you will need to size it first. Mattress sizes are regulated by trade standards and are summarized in the following chart:

Common Bed Name	Width	Length
Crib	28"	52"
Twin or Single	39"	75"
XL-Twin or XL-Single	39"	80"
Double or Full	54"	75"
Queen	60"	80"
Standard King	76"	80"
California King	72"	84"

Once you have determined the size of your mattress set, look for the manufacturer's information. This will be on a tag that is sewn onto the mattress. Many people prefer brand names when buying mattresses, so this information should definitely be included in any advertisements that you make. Also, determine if there are any special attribute to the mattress such as it being a pillow top mattress or made from a special motion absorbing foam.

To price the mattress, you should look at local classifieds for a mattress that is similar to yours, and see how much similar mattresses are selling for at discount mattress retailers. From these figures, determine a price that you think is reasonable, but will allow you a healthy profit.

Motor Vehicles & Trailers

Motor vehicles and motor vehicles accessories such as trailers are often offered at auctions. For some reason, many people feel that once their vehicles are in storage, they have no further need of them and abandon them. This can be a great source of profit for the beginning auctioneer. It really depends on what you find.

Cars are often an exception to the rule about inspecting items before the auction begins. You often will be allowed to look over cars. Most of the time the keys to the car will not be present when a vehicle is sold. This means that you will not be able to start the vehicle that is being sold. As a result of this, you will only be able to perform a visual vehicle inspection before you make any bids on the car, although I have been permitted to look under the hood. To many people, this can be very intimidating. Also, there are many things that could be wrong with a car that you would not notice from a visual inspection alone. For example, the entire transmission could be ruined or the engine could be seized. No amount of simple looking will detect these two problems.

I have bid on several cars in my career as a storage auction buyer. When I look at a vehicle, I look at everything and ask myself question just like when I look in a storage locker full of boxes. I ask myself what is the condition of the car. I ask myself these questions and more:

- Is the car clean?
- Is there any noticeable damage?
- Was this car in an accident?
- What does the engine compartment look like? Is it clean and does it look well maintained?
- How worn are the tires?
- Does the interior smell?
- How many miles are on the car?
- What is the state of the passenger compartment? Is the upholstery in good condition?

From these questions and any others that seem relevant, you can get a very good picture of what the life of this car has been like. You can determine what condition it is probably, but not necessarily in.

When I am determining the amount of money I am going to bid on the car, I consider the visual inspection I have just performed and what I think I can sell the car for at retail if everything actually is in good shape. I also add on a mechanics inspection and the costs of a tow to the total cost, as well as licensing, before I decide on my bid amount. After all, I need to make sure the car is safe for whoever buys it, and it may not start up right away and I will need to tow it to its new storage location. I usually will bid around one third of what I believe I can sell the car for. I will bid more, but am reluctant to do so. It could be a lemon that is of no use to anyone. Even by bidding a third of what I think the car is worth, I am taking a large risk.

One thing to remember about buying cars is that they may not work at all. Then what do you do? Well, at that point you refer back to the section on scrap metal. A car is, after all, nothing buy a big metal construction. As such, it too can be sold to a metal recycler. A car will generally weigh 1.5-2 tons and will be rated at the lowest grade of metal. However, it can fetch you at least several hundred dollars. If you do the towing yourself, this can be a quick buck in your pocket.

Another step you can take with a dead car is to contact local junkyards in your area. A car whose engine is not running may still have good value for the parts that it contains. Many junkyards will pay good money for newer cars that are in relatively good shape. This means that there is something wrong with them that prevents their sale as a running vehicle, but will provide a good supply of parts for sale. A car that has been in a head on collision will often have many useful parts on the back half. To sell a car like this, you will need a title.

If the car you have bought is in running condition, there are several steps you need to take before selling it. The first, if you plan to sell the car, you will need to obtain a title. To do this, visit your state's department of motor vehicles or licensing department. Make sure to take all of the documentation you were give at the time of the auction with you to prove you are the legal owner. With this you should be able obtain a salvage title or abandoned vehicle title. The specifics of this title will depend on your state's laws and regulations. You may also need to submit the vehicle to a state police safety inspection prior to receiving your title. This will verify the vehicles safety to the state's standards as well as verify that the Vehicle Identification Number has not been altered in any way. This is to prevent the trafficking in stolen vehicles and is a step taken for your protection as well. Once the state is satisfied, you will be issued a title to the car. Receiving the title may take up to eight weeks.

The next step that you must take is to get a key made for the vehicle. This is an optional step and is silly unless you are planning to sell the car as a car to be driven. If you decide that this step is appropriate, you can contact a locksmith in your area. They can make a key for the car for you and provide you with as many copies as you are willing to pay for. Armed with a key and a title, you are ready to sell.

To determine the pricing for a particular car in your possession, there exist online price guides. You can find these by searching for "car price guide" in any online search engine. These websites make excellent resources that I have used many times. With them, you can determine geographically relevant prices for your particular make and model. You can also personalize the pricing by being able to add specifics about your car such as mileage, stereo equipment, overall physical condition, tires, etc. This helps to make the results of the price enquiry all the more relevant and gives you a very good place to start with your pricing.

To actually sell a car, there is really no better place than the Internet. You can take advantage of the free local classifieds that I have mentioned so many times before again to sell your car. However, there are also websites that offer specialized advertising services for cars exclusively. These can be worth considering as well. Many of these services will charge you a flat fee to sell your car on their site, no matter how long it takes. This is a great option for bcontrolling your costs during a sale and is an option well worth considering.

Boats

Boats are a great find in a unit and are as much sought after as cars. One time, I was digging though a unit that I had bought. The unit was big and it had taken me two days to get everything out of it. When I finally reached the back wall there was a large dusty bundle in the back corner. I was tired and wasn't really in the mood to unravel everything so I threw it in the truck. Later, when I was unpacking, I found a very nice French made inflatable boat. The boat was 10 feet long and had a fixed mounting point for a motor. I later found out that similar boats sell for about $1000.

This was an inflatable boat and there were no requirements to transfer a title, so the boat was easily sold. However, this is not the case with rigid boats. They are governed under many of the same regulations that govern cars. If you are fortunate enough to purchase a boat at auction, contact your state's department of licensing and explore what you need to do to transfer ownership of the abandoned boat to yourself.

This was really my only experience purchasing a boat, and it was a surprise. Boat buying is not for the novice or something to be done on a whim. There are many specifics that go into a boat's value and these are only understood by someone familiar with boats. For example, the construction material of a boats hull has a huge impact on the resale price you can hope for. A wooden hull can easily be full of dry rot and not be perceptible on a cursory inspection. Unless you are one of those people who are familiar with boats, or feel like taking a real gamble, I would avoid paying large sums for any boats.

If you do, however, find a boat among your purchases, you will need to find out what the boat is worth. Boats will come with plaques attached to their hull that identify their manufacturer as well as the model number and serial number. With this information, you can find relevant used boat prices with online boat price guides. Look for them using similar techniques to those you used to find used car price guides. If the boat is more than a simple fishing boat, you may consider seeking the help of a boat dealer or broker. Their experience and knowledge will help fill the gaps in your own.

This boat was tucked away in the back of a storage unit. New boats like this one often sell for as much as $1000!

Again, the easiest and often fastest way to sell a boat is through the online classifieds. These will allow you to quickly make known what you are selling and how much you are selling it for. There are also specific sites that are dedicated to the sale of boats exclusively. Lastly, if the boat you find is in good condition, you can consign it to a boat dealer for them to sell for you. This of course will cost a percentage of the total sale price.

Musical Recordings

There are two types of musical recordings that are of interest to you as a storage auction buyer. These are CDs and records. Tapes are, unfortunately, not highly sought collectibles and have little value in my experience.

CDs are highly sought after by music enthusiasts. While you can now download and play music on an MP3 player, many people prefer to buy CDs. They like the cover art, and liner notes and look at these as part of the art of music.

Records are a whole different ball park. Many people out there are record enthusiasts. They appreciate the art that was the record and prefer to listen to music on vinyl recordings. People who collect records are usually very specific in the way that they collect these items and what types of music they want.

Even a small collection of records can fetch a surprisingly high price. Don't overlook these items when you are sorting through your new acquisitions.

There are several ways to sell CDs. You can always list CDs on online auctions. Again, because of the small value of these items you may find it difficult to sell them. If I am using an online classified to sell CDs, again I will group them together to make the sale easier.

Online auctions and websites that deal in used media are a good place to sell individual CDs and records. Make sure what you are accurately representing what you are selling. Music recording collectors are very picky and you can quickly earn bad feedback if you are selling items that are not the exact item they are represented to be.

The last place that I will sell CDs and records is at a used music store. These are not uncommon by any means. Many people prefer to shop for their music in these stores because of the lower prices of used music and the availability of hard to find music recordings. These stores will want to make a profit on their purchases and as a result will offer you a lower price than you could get by selling the recordings on your own. However, again, it is sometimes nice to make a fast buck on a quick sale and these stores are a great help with that.

Antiques

I am not an expert on antiques. I am far from it. I have little experience with antiques. However, I know where to do further research and how to find more information on an item. This has come in handy in the past. For example, one unit that I bought had a very dusty box of rusted and painted pieces of metal. Upon closer inspection these pieces were identified as Victorian period heat registers that were manufactured in 1888! Classic hardware of this type is worth a great deal of money.

These two pieces of seemingly worthless junk turned out to be two valuable pieces of Victorian period hardware.

My only real advice when dealing with antiques is that if you think it is old and valuable, look carefully over the who piece for any markings. These can be very small, so look carefully. Once you have found a marking, enter it in an Internet search engine and see what comes up. If the piece is valuable, you should be able to tell from the first listings.

If you can find no markings, and you still think an item is valuable, try visiting your library. There are books about any type of antique you can imagine and these can be a very good resource. These books should be able to help you identify whatever it is that you think you have.

Using online auctions as a means to find the value of an item in your possession is a technique that I have used many times. What I do is simple. I go to an online auction site and begin to browse. Say for example, I have a cigarette lighter that I think was made in Occupied Japan. Well I will start looking though the auctions and refining my search as I go. Ultimately, I am likely to find something that closely matches the item sitting on my desk. At that point, I can learn a great deal about the item from the auction. I can also see what the item is selling for. Armed with this information, I can sell the item, or look in new places for more information. Either way, I am better of than I was.

As a last resort, try visiting an antiques dealer. See what they think. Most of these people will be happy to help you and truly enjoy talking about antiques and will happily share their knowledge. There is a small percentage that might try to take advantage of your ignorance. Be cautious about anyone who quickly offers to buy something from you before you truly know what it is. They may be trying to take advantage of your ignorance.

Pornography

I find boxes of pornography in at least half of the units that I buy at auction. Often the pornography is lying out in plain sight when the unit is sold. Unfortunately, because there is such a large supply of it, pornography is just not a very good item to resell and it is hard to make any money on it. Now, most of the pornography I have found is the discount VHS or DVD variety that is commonly sold in convenience stores and adult bookstores.

That is not to say, because it has nudity in it, it is worthless. Quite to the contrary, certain "gentleman's magazines" are highly sought after collectibles and these can fetch good prices. Also, certain adult movies with well known celebrity performers are widely collected by their fans and can also be sold.

However, most of the pornography you find will be cheap and common and not worth the time to try and sell. At this point, you have three choices; you can throw the porn out, try and sell it as a lot or keep it for your personal collection.

If you do decide to try and sell any pornography finds, try using online classifieds or online auctions. These are your best bet. One note of caution with online auctions is to make sure that you are in compliance with all listing policies before you list you ad. Some auction houses have special rules dealing with adult oriented material such as pornography.

Drugs

It is a sad fact that in this world, people abuse prescription drugs and also see fit to use illegal nonprescription drugs as well. It is also a sad fact that these substances turn up in storage lockers fairly often. I have encountered them more than my fair share of times.

You have two options when you encounter an illegal substance, or similar paraphernalia. You can either dispose of it appropriately, or you can call the police.

In most cases, if I find a bag of pills or marijuana, I will simply flush it down the toilet. If you are uncertain that this is legal, consult with your attorney before doing anything. At all times, you must make sure that you are in compliance with local and federal laws.

Some finds, such as a methamphetamine lab (I have run into this as well) should be immediate cause for calling the police. Certain chemicals used in the production of these drugs can be extremely dangerous and can result in explosions or cancer later down the road. State and local police are properly trained to deal with this hazard and can make sure that you and the local community remain safe. This is of paramount concern.

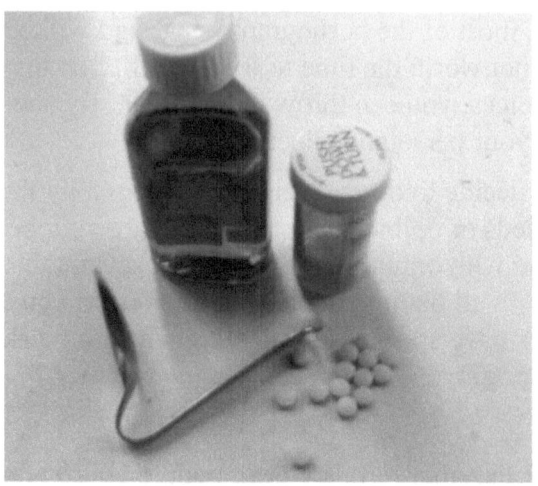

Drugs and drug paraphernalia of any kind should be immediately and safely destroyed or turned over to local police.

This should go without saying, but you never know. <u>Never under any circumstances should you ingest any substances that you find in a storage unit that you have bought.</u> <u>You just do not know what it is and there is no sense in putting yourself at risk.</u> <u>It is not worth it.</u>

Personal Items

People store all kinds of personal items in mini storage lockers. If you buy a unit, you buy everything inside that unit including those personal items. That being said, the storage companies will require you to return all personal items to them for return to the renters. In most states this is a courtesy, however, in some states, you are required by law to perform this duty.

An example will help to clarify the idea of returning personal items. Say for example, you buy a unit that contains a family portrait in an exquisite antique frame. You are required to return the picture; however, the frame is yours under the terms of the sale. The same could be said for a family album. The album is yours but the pictures should be returned.

Personal items that you are required to return in most cases include, but are not limited to:

- Pictures and portraits
- Bank statements
- Pay stubs

- Tax returns

- Mortgage papers

- Legal documents

- Bills, statements, and invoices

As a new buyer you may be tempted to return lots of items that you think are personal in nature. Your instincts and most people's will be to return items that are of no value to you to the people who will value it. Just because they fail to pay their rental bill does not mean that they do not deserve their family memories. The first time I bought a unit, I filled eight large fruit boxes with items that I thought were of a personal nature. I wanted to make sure that I was in compliance with the rules of the storage company so that I could participate in the future. The boxes we filled with all the papers listed above as well as many other items I thought were of a personal nature. However, when I went to return these boxes to the storage company, they took one look at the contents and told me that most of it was not deemed personal. They sorted through and reduced the eight boxes to two. I was told that I would have to dispose of the rest however I saw fit.

The reason for this is simple. Storage companies have lots of auctions and are flooded with personal items. They are sometimes required by law to store these items for a fixed period of time to give the former tenants a chance to return and claim their items. This responsibility takes up space that could otherwise be rented out. As a result, companies want to keep the amount of personal items being stored to a bare minimum to allow them to rent the maximum amount of space to paying tenants.

If you are uncertain as to what items you should return, discuss the specifics with the property manager after you have won a unit at the auction. If you find something after the fact that you think would qualify as a personal item, take it back and ask their opinion. They will appreciate your attention to details in this matter and it will help foster a perception of professionalism and respect on your part.

Junk

People store all kinds of junk in storage units. Why they do it, I honestly do no know. When I mean junk, I mean piles of cardboard, and boxes of wire coat hangers. Additionally, I have found lots of food stored in storage units as well. By this I mean, half opened bags of flour and have empty bottles of white vinegar. When you think about the rent that must be paid each month by a person to store items of this nature it becomes almost crazy.

I try to avoid even taking this stuff to where I store my purchases. They just take up room there and become a headache. Get rid of this stuff as quickly as you can. You will thank yourself in the future.

Items like cardboard and metal can be easily recycled. If you live in an area that permits fireplaces, don't hesitate to burn any cardboard you find. It will help to heat your house and eliminate a silly problem all at once.

Where food is concerned, you have two options. If someone has stored a large supply of nonperishable food, like canned vegetables, you can always donate these to a shelter. This will help their work and solve a problem of yours. If the food is opened, throw it away as quickly as possible. It will attract pests, if it has not already and may cause more trouble than you want.

Conclusion

The items specified in this chapter are really only a scratch on the surface of the types of items that you may find inside storage units that are bought at auction. People have found chests full of gold coins and poisonous snake collections and even body parts! Anything that people own can wind up in a storage unit. No matter what you find, do your homework and investigate your findings carefully to determine its value. Use your community library and other resources like the Internet.

Once you have determined an items value, get down to the business of selling it. Use the tools and techniques presented in this chapter and don't hesitate to use your own instincts to develop new ones. The sky is really the limit!

Afterword

The storage auction business is really a fascinating one. There is really never any telling what types of treasures you may find in a unit that you have purchased. This really adds an air of speculation and a dash of fun to the auction environment.

This business is really very easy to get into. Simply show up one day with cash in hand and start bidding. You might not win anything right off the bat but stick with it and be persistent and eventually you will win a unit and get to go exploring.

In this book we talked about a number of ways to go about turning your treasures into cash in your pocket. I really don't want any of my readers to feel that these are the only methods at their disposal. These are tools that have worked for me in the past and have served me well. However, as I have admitted many times in the pages of this work, I am by no means an expert on anything. You may possess insight that I do not and hopefully, you will build on some of the ideas in this book and come up with new methods. If you do, please write to me care of the publisher. I would love to hear what experiences and fun stories you gain as a result of this work.

I have had many, many days of fun treasure hunting in storage units that I have bought and I wish you all the best of luck. Lastly, thank you very much for your purchase and reading of this work. Good luck!

-Edward Busoni

Check Out These Other Great Titles From Pratzen Publishing
Available at www.pratzenpublishing.com

Fundamentals Of Offshore Banking: How To Open Accounts Almost Anywhere

By Walter Tyndale

This book explores the global banking industry. Inside the covers you will find information on why you might want to open an account in a foreign country, how to do so, and advice on how to protect your deposit. Additionally, many of the countries that will accept foreign deposits are profiled with information about banking regulators and institutions.

$19.95

How To Live A Debt Free Life: Get Out Of Debt And Stay Out Of Debt

By Peter Wilmore

Learn how to free yourself from debt forever inside the pages of this book. The author of this book overcame his own debt and explains how through common sense and careful money management, you can too. In addition, there are chapters about starting to invest for retirement and how to protect yourself and family with insurance.

$19.95

Bartending Basics: A Complete Beginner's Guide

By Thomas Morrell

This book is a how-to guide written by ten year veteran of the restaurant and bar industry. Inside you will learn all about beer, wine and distilled spirits, as well as bartending techniques, ways to remember recipes, responsible bartending, cost and crowd control. There is also a chapter about how to put together a resume and how to find a job to start your new career.

$19.95